RELIGION A CURSE,

RELIGION A DISEASE,

RELIGION A LIE

RELIGION A CURSE,

RELIGION A DISEASE,

RELIGION A LIE.

Dedicated to the American Congress which for the sake of Religion Has Stabbed Liberty to the Heart,

BY SAMUEL P. PUTNAM.

GYAN

Published by

Gyan Publishing House
5, Ansari Road
Daryaganj, New Delhi-110002
Phone: 011-47034999, 9811692060
E-mail: books@gyanbooks.com

Distribution Network
gyanbooks.com
India, USA, Canada, UK, Australia

ISBN: 978-81-212-5685-8 (PB)
First Published, 1893

2nd Impression 2024

Printed at: Gyan Press, Delhi.

RELIGION A CURSE, RELIGION A DISEASE, RELIGION A LIE
Author: SAMUEL P. PUTNAM

RELIGION A CURSE
RELIGION A DISEASE
RELIGION A LIE.

RELIGION A CURSE
RELIGION A DISEASE
RELIGION A LIE.

By

Samuel P. Putnam

RELIGION A CURSE, RELIGION A DISEASE, RELIGION A LIE.

I.

WHATEVER may be the essence of religion it inevitably manifests itself in a belief in God. Exclude all idea of a deity and there is no support for religion. A belief in immortality is the logical result of a belief in God. It is impossible to believe in God, that is, in infinite goodness, without believing in immortality. If the mind is restricted to this present world there is no possible demonstration of deity. Time is perfectly atheistical, absolutely godless. It is only by the reflected light of eternity that any divinity is discoverable. Against the overwhelming logic of the ills that flesh is heir to: of the tragedies of life, of the horrors of human experience, the theologian only finds refuge in the endless hereafter. Without a supernal world he is *hors de combat*. He must give his God another chance, or even he himself is compelled to admit that God is a failure. St. Paul declared that if this life were all then are we most miserable, thus frankly confessing that without immortality the deity is a stupendous fraud. And right St. Paul is, for if you take away from the believer in God the dream of immortality this life becomes to him a terrific puzzle, for he sees his God baffled at almost every point. Certainly the manifestation of God in this life is so weak, so pitiable, so contemptible, so useless, so beggarly, that he needs several eternities in which to vindicate his good name. It will take him a long period hereafter to make up for the infinite wrongs he now permits. I doubt if he ever can prove his omnipotent benevolence—if through millions of eons he can wipe away the stain of his earthly defeat. No amount of deific splendor in the next world might make one fully forgive him his cruel derelictions in this. The only plea that one can possibly make is that of "no jurisdiction;" that this is the devil's world, and the devil will give God no chance. God is "conspicuous by his absence," so far as this life goes. Thus religion is forced to a belief in immortality as a supplement to its belief in God. Take away immortality and religion would perish of despair—for it could no longer defend its God at the bar of human reason.

Thus religion ever has and ever will express itself in these two beliefs, God and Immortality—and when I speak of religion I speak of that in man which necessarily and logically affirms these dogmas.

It might be possible to so subtly define religion as to separate it as a feeling from these dogmas, but as a matter of fact this has never been done. No religion has ever existed without a belief in God and Immortality in some form. A simple belief in Immortality without a belief in God does not constitute a religion. I do not consider Spiritualism a religion. It is simply a philosophy. To believe that I exist to-day does not make me religious; to believe that I will exist to-morrow does not make me religious, and so a belief in existence hereafter as a continuation of this existence, provided that belief is based on present experience, does not make one religious. So when I say that religion is a curse, I do not mean to say that Secular and scientific Spiritualism is a curse, or even a folly. It is simply a human natural belief like a belief in continued life on this planet, and does not involve religion. If Spiritualism does become a religion by insisting upon a belief in God, then it is not only a folly but a curse, and must perish in the pathway of civilization. There are Spiritualists and Spiritualists. The Secular Spiritualist is with us, the religious or godly Spiritualist is against us.

One on evidence can believe in a future life without believing in God; but one cannot believe in God without believing in a future life, but a belief in a future life on a theistic basis is entirely different from a belief in a future life on a natural basis.

Therefore in what might be called common-sense Spiritualism there is no such thing as religion.

There is no such thing as a "Religion of Humanity." Comte has failed in his efforts. There might be a theology without a religion; but there cannot be a religion without a theology. Religion involves worship; for if one believes in a God, he will worship that God. But one cannot worship humanity. There are noble qualities or attributes in humanity; but one cannot worship a quality, or an attribute. He must worship a being. Comte endeavored to make a supreme being out of humanity. But there is no such thing. Humanity is composed of individuals, and the individual being is to our experience the greatest being. Put a million individuals together, and you do not increase the quality of their being. There is no added dignity. You have no supreme being, only the individual still. Hence the worship of humanity is simply the worship of some individual, and such worship is degrading, and of course contrary to the idea of Comte. Comte as a matter of fact invented a huge abstraction, which is after all only a kind of God and has no real existence. Comte rejected theology, but accepted its outer habiliments, its husks; but religion cannot feed upon these, and hence the "religion of humanity" is dead.

The sentiment of humanity is something entirely different from the "religion" of humanity. The sentiments of love, devotion, self-sacrifice, exist in and of themselves, and require no religious foundation. When I speak against religion, I do not speak against a single natural sentiment of humanity. I want to distinguish religion from all these.

Spencer's "religion of the unknowable" is also an absurdity. Religion is not a thought, I grant, but a feeling. But feeling is founded on sensation, and sensation must involve knowledge. In order to feel anything you must sense it, and therefore to feel anything in regard to the "unknowable" one must "sense" it, and if one senses the "unknowable" then he must have some knowledge of it. The infant can give no intellectual definition of its means of sustenance, but will anyone affirm that to the childish mind the breasts of the mother are "unknowable?" As well assert that the sustenance of poetry is unknowable to the poet's, as that the sustenance of religion is unknowable to the believer's, mind. The poet cannot always explain the origin of his ineffable ecstasy, but will anyone affirm that it originates in absolute ignorance? If there is in this universe such a thing as the "unknowable" we cannot possibly conceive it, or picture it, and there ore we cannot possibly have any feeling concerning it, and therefore there can be no "religion of the unknowable."

The endeavor to save religion to science or humanity is absolutely useless. It cannot be done. The curse cannot be taken from religion by seeking to change its nature, or its meaning.

In affirming that religion is a curse—not incidentally, but essentially—it is necessary that we know what religion is. The tree is known by its fruits, and in this way we must know religion.

Religion is inseparable, as I have said, from the God-idea.

What is the God-idea?

I do not see how it is possible to understand God in any other sense than as a personality. An "impersonal God" is a contradiction in terms. The "God of nature" if it means anything more than force means a person. If you call it "purpose," "intelligence," "mind," or even only "tendency," it must still be a personality. If there is a choice in the "tendency" it must be a personal choice. If there is no choice, then why call it God? It is no more "God" than the running of water downhill is "God." Pantheism if it means anything must mean that the whole universe is the expression of a personality. How can pantheism be any different from Atheism if it does not mean this? Atheism recognizes universal force, but that force is neither good nor evil as universal. It is only good or evil when partially considered—that is, when it is in relations. But pantheism asserts that the universal force is good. How can it be good in any real sense except it chooses to be good? How can it be worthy of any reverence unless its goodness is the result of a personal effort? In other words, pantheism simply means that all force is thought-force or will-force, and it is this which Atheism denies. There can be no will-force, however, without a personality.

God therefore, however vaguely and variously the term may be used, is a personality.

There can be no religion therefore without a belief in a personal God, or at any rate in a personal manifestation of God like Christ or Buddha in which is centered the religious feeling and hope.

There is no religion without some supernatural being as the object of its worship.

With these explanations let me a give a definition

of religion which I believe to be perfectly historic and scientific.

Religion is that feeling in humanity which always results in a belief in God, in a personal God or a personal manifestation of God; and also results in a belief in immortality as necessary to the vindication of the justice and goodness of God; and it also results necessarily in worship, in order to obtain the good will of God as the supreme ruler, and to enjoy the rewards of the hereafter, wherein the perfections of God will be victorious.

I propose to show that religion, thus defined, with its attendant results is a curse to humanity, and therefore should be utterly abolished. It is a purely savage feeling, a barbaric belief, and unfit for man's highest civilization. It is the foe of liberty and the enemy of human progress. History proves this, and analysis of the feeling as such will declare why it has been so.

Desperate attempts have been made to save the name of religion, as if religion in itself were a precious jewel—only it has been "in the rough," they say; in bad company and has never shown its pure brilliancy. Clear religion, it is said, of its unfavorable surrounding and it will be a beautiful thing—a benefit to humanity. Religion is not a jewel. It is a dagger—a bloody dagger. It is a dagger in its very nature. Brighten it up and it will be a dagger still. Wipe off the blood and its dazzling blade is still ready for slaughter. You cannot change that dagger into a jewel to shine in peaceful luster. All the ornaments of religion are but the ornaments of a weapon of death.

It is said that the numberless cruelties of religion are the fruits of its abuse, and not of its real nature. Is it possible that the abuse of a naturally good thing could result in such unmitigated evil? If it could be shown that religion has benefited the race, it might be admitted that the evil it has done was not normal, but abnormal. But religion has never benefited the race—it has never given it one truth, one art, one invention, or one discovery. It has been a murderer and a despot from the beginning. It has slain millions of the human race and has not preserved one single human life. It has always opposed science. It has imprisoned the noblest of mankind; put them to the torture and to death. The dungeon, the cross, the fagot, and the chain have been its constant aids. It is nonsense to say that the abuse of a naturally good thing would result in such infinite havoc. Liberty is a naturally good thing, and the abuse of liberty has been simply terrible; but over against this abuse behold the glory that has been achieved through liberty—the hights that have been won, the genius displayed, the knowledge acquired, the virtues attained. In spite of all abuse liberty has been an infinite blessing. But religion can show no such record as against its dark and bloody deeds. It cannot square the account. It has not a single credit mark. It has been evil, and evil only. Not one virtue has it ever given to humanity—not one ray of light or genuine hope. It has never planted one seed, or reaped one golden harvest. It is in its very nature a curse, and history is my witness. It is impossible for a thing really good to be the source of so much misery. What is so everlastingly bad in its effects must be bad at its fountainhead, and this I affirm.

An effort has been made by many liberal-minded religious people to shift the responsibility from religion to theology. It is theology that is the source of these evils, they say, not religion *per se*. I deny this, and affirm that it is religion itself that is the curse, and not the theology that accompanies it. Theology is the child of religion—its intellectual offspring—but the child is not the criminal, but the father. If the child is cruel, it is because the father is cruel. Religion is the root, and theology is the flower, and the bitterness of the root has ever made poisonous the flower, so that it has breathed destruction.

Theology is a purely intellectual affair, and simply as such is perfectly innocent. The theologian simply as a theologian would no more persecute than the mathematician as a mathematician would persecute. Keep theology entirely within intellectual influences and it would be as gentle as philosophy or poetry, or pure metaphysics. It would be merely a mental amusement careless of acceptance or non-acceptance. It is only when feeling is involved that the *theologicum odium* is aroused. The mathematician would be equally cruel if the same feeling co-existed with his mental operations. If the eternal happiness of the mathematician was endangered by a non-belief in the theorem that the square of the hypothenuse is equal to the sum of the square of the other two sides of a triangle, he would instantly persecute everyone who would not accept the theorem. Or if he was convinced that a denial of this theorem was necessary to his eternal happiness, he would not only deny it himself, but draw the sword and compel everybody else to deny it, and imprison and kill those who affirmed it. The purely intellectual man would never persecute, be he theologian or mathematician; but when his intellect becomes the slave of feeling then the spirit of persecution is aroused. Religion the feeling, and not theology the intellectual perception, has been the source of every persecution, and it is absurd to try to vindicate religion at the expense of theology. It won't do. Neither history, nor science, nor human nature admits the evasion. Theology has been hideous and damnable, but it is religion that has made it so. Take away religion and theology would sink into "innocuous desuetude." It would then become an intellectual toy—a plaything of the imagination, a will-o'-wisp of the fancy. But join religion with theology and it is at once a cruel beast, like its progenitor.

If I bring theology to the bar of human judgment, I bring it simply as the accomplice of religion. Religion is the instigator of every crime which theology has sanctioned. Theology has simply followed after; it has not gone before. Religion is the master, theology is the perpetual slave. Kill religion and you will kill theology; but kill all present forms of theology and new forms will appear, still partaking of the dark and bitter fountain from whence they spring. It is useless to fight theology merely. It is religion itself that must be exterminated, and then theology will trouble us no more.

It is said that religion is a beautiful thing. So is the tiger beautiful when it is not mad. What is more beautiful than its graceful antics? So is the serpent beautiful when it is not angered. What is more charming than a snake? What glorious colors it has. What delightful movements. What exquisite grace. But the nature of the tiger and the snake exist in spite of their beautiful appearances. Yes, religion is beautiful, wonderfully attractive. It charms the eye and ear. Behold its gorgeous temples, its majestic statues, its enchanting pictures, its gloom irradiant with colors soft and thrilling. Listen to its solemn music, its chants, its sweet songs, its alluring voices. Yes, religion is beautiful. Its service is magnificent. It awes and subdues. The worshipers bow with rapture. Yes, religion untouched seems as peaceful as a poetic dream—it flows along a limpid shining stream—and who could think for a moment that there could be any terror in this lovely apparition, that it could torture and slay, that it was more cruel than the grave, that its music could turn to groans—its songs to tears—its temples to dungeons?

Ah, the ocean is beautiful, beautiful in its sunny glory, beautiful as it breaks in white splendor all along the sunny beach, beautiful in its calm blue depths beneath the calm blue sky, beautiful as it flows against the silver morn or golden eve; beautiful as the ship speeds merrily over its azure plain; beautiful as the stars are mirrored in its soft expanse; beautiful as it mingles with the moonlight on dark-browed rocks; beautiful as the chambered nautilus sails along its diamond surface; beautiful as we daintily play with its glittering billows, and the boat rocks to our happy dreams and the far off horizon seems like Cleopatra's jewel melting in the glorious effulgence of the purple of the sea. Oh, it is beautiful, but let the breast of that peaceful ocean be smitten by the storm, let the hurricane come, where is the beauty then? Lost in terror, in shipwreck, and in death. Then everywhere the sea becomes a raging monster; it lashes the shores, it hurls thousands to destruction; it is an immeasurable horror.

So with religion, beautiful when summer's peace is brooding over it, but let religion be struck with fear, let it feel that its pomp and power are endangered, that it must preserve itself, and it becomes a monster, it fights like the wild beast, it bites like a serpent. It rends, it tears, it crushes, it devours, it kills. It is like the mighty ocean when the whirlwind is sweeping over it. Its beauty vanishes in immeasurable gloom. Then the tiger, the serpent nature of this beautiful religion is revealed.

It does not seem as if a belief in God and immortality could be so cruel. How can a belief in infinite goodness make one infinitely devilish? How can a belief in eternal existence kindle the fires of dark damnation? Yet it is so. These two beliefs have been the most dangerous in all human history. Dominating the mind, intensely held, they have transformed man to a tiger. It is strange that what appears so beautiful in itself, so sublime and precious, should be the source of the greatest horrors. One would think that a belief in God would make one kind and charitable. That the dream of immortality would suffuse life with measureless sweetness. But these beliefs have had the exactly opposite effect. Regarded as the greatest of blessings they have really been the greatest of curses. It is religion that has made them so. If these beliefs had been purely scientific they would indeed have been a "thing of beauty and a joy forever." If God and Immortality had been the gifts of science, how noble they would have been, how infinitely splendid. What warmth and brilliance they would have shed on human life. What grace and magnificence they would have given to human toil. But being, not the gifts of science but the creatures of religious feeling, they have been a bloody paraphernalia along man's pathway. The face of God has been the face of a fiend, and the dream of immortality an eternal hell.

This is simply a fact, attested by a thousand wars, a million murders. I will endeavor to explain this fact and show that religion in its very nature must be cruel.

Religion originates in a desire for happiness. It

is not that desire simply in itself, but the intensification, the crystallization, the abnormal emphasis of that desire. It is that desire made determinate, all-absorbing and all-commanding.

The very nature of religion therefore is absolute selfishness. It originates in selfishness. It is the expression of selfishness. From beginning to end it is a colossal egotism. It is more selfish than the desire for food by the hungry man, or for warmth by the naked wanderer.

How often it has been declared that religion is self-sacrificing; that it is indeed in its very essence self-sacrifice. There never was a falser idea; there never was an act of religion that did not pertain to self; that did not begin with self and end with self. There is not a particle of generosity, of self-abandon, of real kindness in religion. Religion sacrifices I admit, always sacrifices, but it never sacrifices self. It sacrifices a lesser good to a higher—the little self to the larger self—that is all. Self is not forgotten or obliterated. Religion has been one long record of sacrifices—sacrifices of millions of men, of doves, of sheep, of oxen, of the fruits of the earth. Religion is nothing but sacrifice, we might say, but never self-sacrifice. I challenge the production of one single deed of real self-sacrifice in all human history that has been the result of the religious motive. Great acts have been done for religion's sake—acts of heroism and splendor, romantic acts—but these acts have been all for the glory of the self Armies have been led to mighty battles, innumerable sufferings have been borne. dangers dared, death encountered, for religion's sake, still the ulterior motive has been the exaltation of self.

The simple desire for happiness is perfectly right and innocent, and when pursued in an equable way without making, as Dickens says, any fuss about it; taking it as it comes with a sort of wise carelessness, letting it flow like a crystal stream in regardless beauty, and not damming it up into a huge motive power which constantly and distinctly appears—pursued in this fashion, not directly, but indirectly, the desire and the attainment of happiness are a perpetual benefit. Reason, philosophy, and science thus regard happiness. It is incidental to human effort and not its absolute goal.

Of course we must be happy; but the best way to be happy is to spend but little thought about it. We labor and are happy; but if we labor to be happy we are very apt to be miserable. Happiness is so subtle a spirit that it evades direct search and drops upon the unconscious mind.

The method of religion is not the method of reason, science, and philosophy. Religion accentuates the desire for happiness, fondles it, cultivates it, and makes it a supreme desire. It becomes more than a desire—it becomes a purpose—a conscious effort, an ultimate aim. Religion not only wants happiness, but eternal happiness, an assured happiness that even time cannot destroy. Religion is a searching after happiness, and the being who is supposed to grant happiness becomes the object of passionate worship. The cry of religion is, "I want to be happy," and that is the curse of religion, because in its effort after happiness it crushes and it kills, as the wild beast crushes and kills in its efforts to satisfy hunger. All that religion has ever done in this world, with its beliefs, its worships, its rituals, its temples, its sacrifices, its wars, its persecutions, for the attainment of happiness, has been a tremendous failure. It ever will be a failure, misery instead of bliss. Religious people are not only unhappy in themselves, but they make everybody else unhappy. Religion becomes by the very pursuit after happiness a most solemn affair, a melancholy procedure. Even the most excruciating sufferings are invented and endured in order that the exquisite bliss of the final reward may be greater. What has not been done for religion's sake? Its votaries have lived naked in the desert, have given up every earthly comfort, have plunged the knife into their own flesh, have walked on hot irons, have whipped their bleeding bodies, have stood in one posture for years on the bare sands or the fiery column, have poured by the million into the battle's cruel front, and all for the sake of happiness, "eternal happiness." In no other way can one explain the awful phenomena of religion. At the heart of it is an exaggerated desire for happiness, for a happiness so secure and so brilliant that the fluctuations of time cannot disturb its eternal glory. Most of the enormous miseries of man have been created and endured through this desire for happiness. What a satire on the folly of human nature. The very desire for happiness has been the fruitful source of unnumbered woes. How much better off man would have been had he never made so much fuss about his "soul's salvation." If he had taken things as they are, with moderation, accepted the happiness which follows after, not sought that which is before and ever flitting, what a paradise he might have attained. At any rate, what an immense amount of suffering and error would have been avoided.

The simple desire for money is not only innocent, but beneficial. Everyone should desire money. It is a good thing. One cannot be without it, and should labor for it. But the desire for money should be moderate. It should not be an all-absorbing passion. Money in itself is a blessing, but when made the goal of all human effort it becomes a curse. Who is more contemptible than the miser? Who is a greater fool? Who so misses the very essential value of money? To live and dream and hope with only money in view; to bend every energy to its acquisition, is to destroy the very purpose for which money exists. What is the use of money to the miser? It is absolutely useless, and in fact, it ceases to be money. The miser's greed is for money, and yet his very greed when he gets the money destroys its value as currency—that is, its real value as money. The very desire for money changes money from coin to a useless burden.

The religious man is simply a miser—the miser of happiness. By his very miserliness he loses the thing he wants. The natural desire for happiness becomes unnatural. Nature ceases to gratify his enormous passions and he resorts to that which is above and beyond nature. He resorts to God and to Immortality. Only these can satisfy his inordinate craving. Time for him is bankrupt. Eternity alone can redeem his claims. Hence he sacrifices the pleasures of this world, the happiness that is attainable, the every-day joys and comforts of earthly existence, for a transcendent bliss beyond the grave. As the miser in his greed never gets the real value of money, so the religious man in his greed never gets the value of the life that actually is. He wants to be so happy that he isn't happy at all.

The belief in God is therefore a purely selfish belief. People believe in God because they want to believe in one who can make them infinitely happy, and for no other reason. The intellect does not demand God. God explains nothing. The pure intellect abhors God, even as nature abhors a vacuum, for to the pure intellect God is nothing; as the creed says, he is without body, parts, and passions. And what has the pure intellect or science to do with such a nonentity? It is the heart that craves for God. When the desire for happiness becomes supreme, illimitable, then nothing can satisfy that desire but a belief in God, and hence the passionate belief in him—the most selfish belief of man, and so the most cruel belief. The belief in Immortality, as a Theistic belief and orthodox belief, is also an intensely selfish belief, and a cruel belief. As the very essence of religion is selfishness, so the very essence of its two grand doctrines is selfishness, and hence the cursed nature of these doctrines and the cursed nature of religion. And its voice has ever been, "Unless ye hate father and mother, brother and sister, wife and child, yea and your own life also, ye cannot be my disciple." Such is the imperious command of this colossal egotism. What is its God but the reflection of the believer's own self—that which is most dear and beautiful to him—seated on the throne of the universe? What is Immortality but the prolongation and triumph of this inner self above and beyond the wrecks of time? God is the universality of self-Immortality—that is, orthodox Immortality is the eternal victory of self. And it is no wonder that these two beliefs have filled with bloodshed and horror the pages of history; for no hungry beast will fight for food as man will fight for what he considers absolutely necessary to his happiness.

I believe that history, science, a knowledge of human nature, a study of religious literature, an analysis of religious sentiment in all its various manifestations, will justify this definition of religion as the most selfish, and the most cruel, passion of which humanity is capable. That it is the most cruel who will deny? What makes it cruel but its selfishness? That it is potent who will deny? but what makes it potent but the desire for happiness that is in it? That is why it so long endures, although science condemns it. This is why it survives in spite of all its horrors and follies. This is why it is so attractive when no dangers threaten it. This is why it is so furious when it is attacked, why it persecutes, why it imprisons and murders, why it opposes change and progress, new truths and new ideals. It is not a mere doctrine, but a desire, and if a desire then it must be a desire for happiness, but not a simple, natural, moderated desire, which is wisdom and humanity, but an exaggerated, unnatural, all-absorbing desire, whose fruit is inhumanity, ignorance, superstition, slavery, worship, blind faith, suffering, poverty, war, and every curse imaginable. There is no wrong and no injustice of which religion has not been guilty. It has increased a thousandfold the natural misery of mankind. It has not diminished any actual suffering. It has not added to the real happiness of this world any more than the miser has added to the real wealth of the world by his morbid craving. Religion is nothing but selfishness emphasized, crystallized, doctrinized, institutionized, made into a church, a creed, a sword, a dungeon, a rack, a whip, a scaffold. Religion gave the hemlock to Socrates. If the record be true it was religion that hounded Jesus to his death for no other reason than that he was an infidel and a blasphemer, and when afterward the religion of Jesus triumphed it was the bloodiest conqueror of all. It was religion that hurled the wild monks of Africa upon the beautiful naked body of Hypatia, and the rude multitude tore her to pieces with the fury of a mad beast, because she represented that glorious philosophy which is the eternal opponent of religion. Religion destroyed the magnificent library of Alexandria, for books laden with the treasures of human thought are the destroyers of religion. Religion poured a million people upon devoted Palestine, who perished for the sake of heaven and not for the benefit of humanity. In their eyes the victorious cross was the symbol of eternal happiness. Religion invented the ghastly Spanish Inquisition. Was it not better to torture men to death than suffer a soul to be lost? The horrors of the French Revolution were the result of religion, for did not Robespierre say that if "there were not a god it would be necessary to make one?"

Religion has been simply and solely evil, and when the secret of religion is revealed we understand why it has been so incessantly devilish. It is the master egotism of the human heart and it will abide nothing in opposition.

An orthodox preacher, known to be very radical in his views, was asked by a friend of mine why he continued in the pulpit contrary to his intellectual convictions. He pointed to his little child—a lovely girl that might charm the heart of any father—and replied: "For that little girl's happiness I would not only lie, but I would steal!" A father's love is beautiful, but how cruel and unjust it might be. That father's love was a religious love, not a generous, reasonable, moral love: it was a selfish love that would make him a criminal if need be. Such is the spirit of religion. It is a tremendous passion. It is devotion to what the mind thinks most beautiful and dear. But in its very devotion it becomes a hideous madness. As that father for his child, so religion for the sake of the entrancing object of its adoration, would lie and steal and murder—for this it has done all through human history. I challenge the production of one single line in all religious literature that breathes anything but selfishness. Religion says that man is "to glorify God and enjoy him forever." That means that one is to glorify self and enjoy self forever. God is not objective but subjective. Born of the ego, he reflects the ego. I do not care how beautiful the idea of God may be it is still self, and therefore the very dearest thing for which the self can strive.

I never heard an orthodox prayer yet that was not purely selfish. I never heard an orthodox sermon that was not an appeal to pure selfishness. I never heard a Christian hymn that was not the very outbreathing of absolute egotism.

While writing this essay I attended an orthodox revival-meeting, and the first hymn sung with the usual fervor was the following:

> How sweet the name of Jesus sounds
> In a believer's ear;
> It soothes his sorrows, heals his wounds,
> And drives away his fear.
>
> It makes the wounded spirit whole,
> And calms the troubled breast;
> 'Tis manna to the hungry soul,
> And to the weary rest.
>
> Dear name, the rock on which I build,
> My shield and hiding-place,
> My never-failing treasure—filled
> With boundless stores of grace

Jesus, my shepherd, savior, friend;
  My prophet, priest, and king;
My Lord, my life, my way, my end,
  Accept the praise I bring.

I would thy boundless love proclaim
  With every fleeting breath;
So shall the music of thy name
  Refresh my soul in death.

I leave it to anyone who understands human emotion if this is not the expression of a purely selfish emotion. Where is the self-sacrifice in this hymn? There's not a bit of it. It is the very passion of egotism. Substitute "Almighty Dollar" for the name Jesus, and not a sentiment would need to be altered. The same emotion would burn in the heart. The only difference is that Jesus in the long run gives more happiness than the dollar. If the dollar could guarantee as much glory hereafter as in this world Jesus would be nowhere. Jesus has the advantage of eternity, and hence his superior attractions. This is a model Christian hymn, and yet what is it but the outpouring of gratitude for favors received and flattery for favors expected? Is there anything in that hymn that a courtier wouldn't say to his king?

There is self-abasement in religion, prostration in religion, humility in religion, but not self-sacrifice. Every posture, every attitude, every voice, every lowly act of religion, is for self. It is for the glorification and enthronement of self. Religion is not a curse because of its abuse. It is a curse because it cannot help being a curse. Every horror that it has made is its legitimate fruit. It is the terrific activity of the most subtle and overmastering egotism of which human nature is capable, a selfishness so enormous that the theater of this world is not sufficient. It must invent a God and Immortality as the only possible means to satisfy its illimitable cravings. How the passion of the miser, of the gambler, of the drunkard, of the glutton, sinks into insignificance in comparison with this gigantic passion that in its vast desires sweeps beyond "the flaming bounds of space and time." No wonder that religion when aroused is such an insatiable destroyer. No wonder that it desolates this fair earth to save its supernatural heaven. No wonder that it is a curse, always a curse, and to-day a curse.

II.

Having shown that religion is a curse, I now propose to show that it is a disease. It might be a curse and still be a natural and universal characteristic of human nature, and therefore permanent; and we could only comfort ourselves with the maxim, "What can't be cured must be endured." But religion is not natural and universal. It does not belong to healthful human nature. It is a disease. It therefore can be got rid of by mental hygiene.

It is said that man is a religious animal. I deny this. Man is not a religious animal any more than any other animal is religious. Religion is the misfortune of man, not a necessity. Man is not born to be religious, any more than he was born to have the cholera.

Religion is not universal. The religious feeling itself is not universal. As a matter of fact it exists in a very small minority of the human race.

Religion has always drawn the sword, and forced itself upon the world, and this is why it has seemed to be in such a big majority. It is as if an insane man should thrust himself upon a whole community and compel everyone to be insane or act as if they were insane.

I grant that immense numbers of mankind are cowards and hypocrites, and this is why religion so far has won the day.

The really religious people have forced the cowards and hypocrites under their banner.

Cowards and hypocrites are not necessarily religious. They only pretend to be. I claim that not one in a hundred is really religious. The human being is naturally Secular. Religion is the aristocracy of fanaticism. A few fanatics have compelled the majority not only into submitting to its dictates but into actually believing that they are religious themselves when they are not so.

Who among the people that we meet with are religious? How many talk religion as they talk politics or literature or science? How many read religious books? The Bible is covered with dust even in Christian homes. In a letter to a friend Charles Sumner said he himself was not a religious man, and could not realize what the religious feeling might be. Sumner was honest, and he represents a very large number of people who are non-religious, and yet they dare not be as frank as Sumner. To confess to a lack of religious feeling seems like confessing to a lack of some natural quality. Such is the power of fanaticism even upon intelligent minds. Religion is something that is put on. It is a profession, an artifice, an imitation, a veneer. In civilized society religion is ignored. If one is really religious and tries to live it and talk it, he becomes a nuisance. By common compact religion is avoided in ordinary conversation. Religion is a supposition, and it is impolite to make it anything more than a supposition. One is supposed to be religious, but no questions must be asked. One can say Good morning and How do you do? and How are the folks? etc., but it won't do to say How's your soul this morning? You would laugh at one who should make the inquiry, and if he persisted you would be indignant.

If a man is religious, he will naturally express himself in that way. It is absurd to say that a truly religious man would keep his feelings to himself. It is the very nature of religion to break out like the small-pox.

There is no "golden silence" in religion. It is noise all the time. Religion never "lets concealment, like a worm in the bud, feed on its damask cheek." It is voluble. It runs to tongue as easily as it runs to ears. Tongues and ears are indicative of true religion. Both are characteristics—lengthwise and all. "He that hath ears to hear, let him hear," is a religious injunction. Also "Preach the gospel to every creature" goes with it. Religion could not subsist without preaching any more than it could subsist without believing. Religion would die if it had to keep still Therefore it is patent that every religious man and woman can be counted. Religion will manifest itself in some sect, however small. The statistics will therefore gather in all the religious people of the country.

The membership and attendance of all the religious sects and churches in this country, of every name, only number a little over twenty-one million. Therefore the non-religious people of this country are in a majority of over two to one—admitting that all the twenty-one millions are religious people. But are they? It will be easily admitted that a large number of hypocrites and cowards are in this twenty-one millions. All the hypocrites and cowards are with the church. I think that universal experience will testify that one-quarter of the human race are hypocrites and cowards. Therefore, fifteen millions of the inhabitants of the United States are hypocrites and cowards. I do not think this an exaggeration. This leaves out of the twenty-one millions only six millions that are honestly religious. I think this a large proportion. I am sure that there are not more than a million really religious people in this country. The country could not stand any more than that number, when we consider what a rampant bigot the truly pious man is. Our safety lies in the fact that only a few are religious, as it lies in the fact that only a few are insane.

These figures clearly prove that religion is not universal. It is partial. It is not natural; it is artificial. It is not health; it is disease.

If we take the church's own figures, less than one-third are religious. Fling out the cowards and hypocrites and less than one-tenth are religious.

An orthodox clergyman recently declared that in the city of Boston there are only thirty thousand regular attendants upon divine service. In New York city only three hundred thousand attend church from Sunday to Sunday. The same proportion holds in every city and in every village. Let anyone consult his own experience as to the number of church-members among his acquaintances; and of these how many are sincerely religious? Religion does not enter into the life of one hundredth part of the people we meet. How many, as Ingersoll says, simply "believe that they believe." A recent church publication declares that only three per cent of the young men of this country are in open association with the churches. I realized this paucity of religion when I was in the ministry. I thought when I left the Theological Seminary, that I certainly was in the "swim," that religion was popular, that the people wanted it. I soon discovered my mistake. The vast majority of the people didn't want religion. The majority of my congregation, and the majority of my supporters, were non-religious. They didn't care a rap for religion. Religious topics were a humdrum affair, not half so interesting as corn and potatoes. I found that secular sermons pleased the people best; plain, simple discourses on morality. Every minister knows this, and it is the burden of his life. How often does he complain of the lack of spirituality, of dull prayer-meetings, etc. How much of the church work to-day is purely literary, and sociable church fairs take the cake and the cash too. Kissing-bees are the fashion. Greet one another with a holy kiss, at twenty-five cents each, is the ritual. Preachers have to ransack newspapers to get subjects to talk about. Sensational titles are the only ones that attract. "Get there," as Sam Jones says, is the theme and spirit of every discourse, and the only way that Sam Jones gets there is to be the "end man" of a minstrel show. The church has to resort to every trick to preserve its staying qualities. Even hell-fire is played out. A scandal in the church choir is a better advertisement than a million golden harps. There is music then and the pews are full. The churches subsist to-day on purely worldly nutriment. Oyster soup does more for the churches than all the prayers of the preachers. The cooking-stove in the fashionable ecclesiastical kitchen is a more effectual calling both to saints and sinners than all the fires of damnation, or the breath of the Holy Ghost. Take the "Sewing Circle," where pious women stitch, stitch for the glory of God. That is the place for religion of course. What an opportunity for the communion of saints, for spiritual edification, for holy conversation. Surely if religion is natural and universal, the sewing-circle should be the scene of its most illustrious presence. Yet religion is not mentioned once in a million times in a sewing-circle. Anything and everything is talked about but religion. Every fashion and every scandal is discussed; but religion is untouched.

These are facts patent to every observer of modern religious life. It is affirmed, however, that civilization itself is artifice; that if you want to deal with real human nature you must go to savage life, the untutored life. This, it is said, is the natural existence, and here you find the natural universal feelings of humanity. To discover what belongs to man *per se*—what is original with him—one must go to primeval man, in close contact with physical nature. Here is man as nature meant him to be, and here religion is an overmastering quality, and therefore it is natural and universal.

There never was a falser idea than the idea that the savage is a more natural man than the civilized man. A careful study of the habits physical and otherwise of savage life will show that there are more artifice, more Mrs. Grundyism, and more unnatural fashions and styles among savages than among civilized people. Civilized people are the most natural people. They live more in accordance with nature than do the savages. Civilized people even live a more outdoor life than savage people. They are in closer, finer, and every way more subtle and fruitful contact with physical nature. They know nature better, they love nature better, and they use nature better. Physical culture among civilized people far surpasses physical culture among savages. The habits of eating are more natural and simple among the former than among the latter. The civilized man can outwalk, outrun, and outswim the savage. He can endure more hardships. Irritating as are the follies of society to-day, they are a vast improvement on the follies of our rude ancestors. Is there anything natural in slitting the nose, boring the ear, daubing the cheek, flattening the head, tattooing the body? Civilization is natural. The art, the poetry, the grace and glory of it, are all natural. We distinguish between art and nature, but art is simply conscious nature, selected nature, nature molded, attuned, made harmonious; but art is evermore nature, Science is nature, and it triumphs only by its devotion to nature, by its unfolding of nature, by translating nature from the partial into the universal. The civilized man and woman are the noblest, freest, and most veritable interpreters of nature.

If religion were natural and universal, what a magnificent blossom it would be in the world's civilization, instead of the weak and puerile thing it is to-day. The verdict against religion therefore is true. A perfect civilization will cast it out, for religion indicates a partial, one-sided, and therefore a diseased condition of humanity.

Read the supreme literature of the world; how little of it is purely religious. I do not remember of one religious character in all Shakspere—that is, one who is actuated by religious motives. The stormy passions of Shakspere are all of this world. God and Immortality play an incidental part in his majestic dramas. It is so even with Homer. His gods are only machinery. It is the men, the heroes, that interest, and not the divinities. The two great religious poets, Dante and Milton, are but little read. Scott is mainly secular. Dickens and Thackeray are altogether so. George Eliot is somewhat religious, but "Adam Bede," which is purely human, is her most popular work. "Robert Elsmere" is read because it shows that religion is dying out and portrays the process. The secular press overpowers the religious press. Art no longer paints angels but men. The theater outranks the church. Christians pay $1 an hour to hear Ingersoll. The popularity of theological books lies in the amount of heresy which they contain. Pure orthodoxy is flung into the wastebasket.

Talmage is a representative of religion, and he appeals for help to save his temple from the auctioneer's hammer. What is the result? Out of all the wealth of this country only $250 per day is collected. That is a gage of the average interest of people in religion. Suppose it were a case of simple human charity, how much more would be contributed? Two hundred and fifty dollars per day out of the millions in circulation is a pretty fair index of the real relation of religion to the universal world.

I believe that if we could get at the heart of savage life we should find that only a few are properly religious, but these few have the knack of ruling the rest. Religion breeds fear, and fear controls. Religion is mainly a pretense and imitation among savages as among ourselves, and we shall find it so in every nation. Religion has been one vast imposition. It has the virulence of a fever and a disease. It is its nature to rule or ruin. It is like drunkenness or insanity. It insists upon a like condition in others. The ancient priest was a medicine man, and all preachers are medicine men to-day. We call them doctors of divinity. They do doctor, but not to lessen the disease but to increase it, for therein is their profit. It won't do to cure, for then religion would vanish, and the doctor have no more patients and no more pay.

Religion is a fungus growth upon humanity. It betokens bad blood. The origin of every religion is a delirium. Thomas Paine says of the Christian religion: "It begins with a dream and ends with a murder." Religion is indeed a dream, but a terrible dream—a nightmare. It must be utterly abolished. Its very beginning is wrong—unnatural. That which is natural, simple, and humane is opposed to it. As St. Paul says the natural man does not want religion. Only the spiritual man—that is, the diseased man. It is the universality of ill health that gives religion its prevalence. The mental hallucination feeds upon bodily ailments.

The very moment we grant that religion is not natural and universal, as facts do declare—as history will declare when rightly understood—we are driven to the conclusion that religion is a disease. In my analysis of religion I have shown why it is a disease, that it is an exaggerated desire—like the miser's desire for wealth—and in that very exaggeration lies the disease. The genesis of religion in the mind is like the genesis of disease in the body. It is an abnormal activity. It is partial and one-sided action. It is too much force expended in one direction. It is a destruction of harmonious balance.

Religion must be treated both as an evil and a disease; not a natural evil, but an evil which man himself has manufactured. Man makes religion as he makes intemperance, and we must treat religion as we treat intemperance. Modern science recognizes intemperance as a disease, and in treating it as a disease we adopt the wisest method of its cure. So with religion. It is something of which we must be cured, no matter how we come by it, through inheritance or otherwise; and we must recognize the necessity of a cure—that it is a disease we are dealing with, and our measures must be sanitary. One cannot get rid of a cancer by treating it as a natural growth, and we cannot destroy religion or its evil effects until we see just what religion is—a curse indeed, as I have fully demonstrated, but a curse in and through the fact that it is a disease and that it is not natural any more than any disease is natural, nor universal any more than insanity is universal. I consider it of the first importance to thus understand religion, for it gives us hope that we can destroy it, root it out, as we root out the seeds of any other disease. We must deal thus radically or we shall never remove its bitter fruit from man's pathway. Religion, whether regarded as an evil or not, has been too long accepted as something native to man. It is not native any more than the cancer or cholera is. It is not a necessary or universal evil. It is not a natural curse. It is a disease immensely fearful. Deep as hell it may be, but it can be cured, and our efforts must lie in this direction. We are not simply to abhor it, we must treat it scientifically, as we treat the cancer and the cholera. The death of religion is the triumph of hygiene.

III.

Having shown that religion is a disease, that it is not natural and universal, but special and artificial, the aggravation and distortion of a simple natural desire, which is what constitutes a disease, as a boil on the human body is the aggravation and distortion of its simple natural elements, I now propose to show that religion is a lie. When I say that religion is a lie I do not mean to say that religion does not exist, that in itself it is nothing. It is too terribly a reality—like other diseases. Religion is a lie because the two great dogmas which itself produces and upon which it flourishes are lies—monstrous lies—namely, God and Immortality. The God-idea and the belief in Immortality do not exist in and of themselves. They are not the natural products of human reason and experience. They would never have existed if man had always been in a perfectly healthful condition. The perfectly healthful man has no need of God or Immortality. These dogmas are the result of disease, the disease of religion, and they are lies. It is commonly thought, I know, that the notions of God and Immortality are original with the human mind and that religion is the result of these notions. I claim that the cause and effect are entirely the other way. Religion is the cause, and God and Immortality are the effects. Religion is fundamental; it is the fountain-head, and the ideas of God and Immortality, church, theology, etc., all flow from this source, and without religion all these would cease to be. All are manifestations of ill health. Every church, every pulpit, every sermon, every prayer, every pope, every bishop, all the pomp and ritual of the temple, all the splendor of the cathedral, the revival, the evangelist, the Salvation Army, the cardinal's red robe, each spectacle from Talmage's mouth to the pope's toe, Moody, Sam Jones, Joe Cook, *et cetera*, are the variable symptoms of a vast disease. Religion is a big. burning boil, preachers are pimples, churches are cancers and piety is pus. I am not to blame for these terms. They are medical.

God and immortality are twin lies. They are born of the same parent. They nourish that parent, and they nourish one another. Neither without the other could survive.

They are lies—pure creatures of human feeling—the offspring of the enormous miseries of human existence. Man is theistic simply and solely because he is unhappy. God is born of agony, of suffering, and of pain—the fiction of the imagination to console the bitterness of man's estate. I do not wonder that men believe in a God, seeing that living in this world is such a furious struggle, and so many go to the wall and hope is lost. Millions are constantly wrecked, and torture of the mind and body, more or less, is the fortune of every human being. In a blind and miserable way people try to escape reality—shut their eyes and dream of heaven. It is like taking an opiate. It weakens, while it cures not the ills of life. It is a desperate resort. It heals not the wound. It sends the poison deeper in.

We must confront reality and make the best of it. By courage we can win something of happiness from our dark surroundings. Only, however, by sticking to the truth. If we abandon truth we are lost indeed.

We must not abuse the intellect—make it a slave to search earth and heaven for some delightful falsehood to soothe and comfort our distress. We must accept facts, no matter how ugly they are. Better be crucified with a fact than rot with some splendid lie.

The pure intellect confronting all this world—its hights and depths, its array of stars, its carpet of flowers, its jeweled seas, its shining mountains, its flaming sun, its ocean of blue, its laws and forces, its gigantic evolutions, its sweeps of light and its bursts of splendor—finds nowhere any God, not a scintilla of evidence. It finds the world, and only the world; nothing outside of the world. It can not pierce beyond and does not wish to pierce beyond. It is satisfied with the world. The world only can explain itself. It is the heart, not the intellect, that seeks after God; for the heart wants not an explanation, but a consolation.

Search the universe; dig into the bowels of the earth; walk in the chambers of the deep; catch the lightning; analyze the finest petal; dissect the human body, the eye, the hand, the beating heart itself; multiply a thousandfold man's glorious vision, and travel among the illimitable stars, and God is not even a shadow. Illuminate man's reason with a million suns and still he knows not God. Leave this muddy vesture of decay, if you will, and stand upon Arcturus's blazing crest; traverse the resplendent spaces while ages wing their flight, and still there is no God. Nor time, nor space reveal him. Nor history, nor science declare him. Poor, helpless God—if there is one—he seems forever imprisoned in his own immensity. He cannot manifest himself at a single point in this crowded universe. Even the worm can do better than that. The worm gives us facts, but God never does. In that respect the worm, the pebble, the sod, the snowflake, the raindrop, surpass God. Think of it, O theologian!

Theology in all its thousand tomes of waste paper has given but one argument in support of its claims, namely the argument from design. Surely if the argument from design cannot demonstrate God's existence no argument can.

But logic overthrows this argument and evolution simply annihilates it.

To prove design you must prove a beginning. You can prove design in a watch or house because you can prove the beginning of a watch and house. But if you could not prove the beginning of a watch or house, you could not prove that there was any design. A designed thing must be a begun thing. Suppose the watch and the house never began to be, suppose they existed eternally, then of course, there would be no design in a watch or house. They always existed exactly as they are. Logic plainly declares—no beginning, no design.

Therefore, unless you can prove the beginning of the universe you cannot prove any design in it. But it is impossible to prove the beginning of the universe. We were not there, and as we were not there, and can't "get there," not even Sam Jones, how can we prove the beginning? This is logic which no one can deny.

Do you assume that because there is design, or adaptation, therefore there was a beginning? That is begging the whole question. It is putting the cart before the horse. No true logician will affirm such a proposition. Design cannot prove a beginning. It is beginning that must prove the design. But grant the proposition that design or adaptation proves beginning. Then if it proves the beginning of the universe, it proves also the beginning of God, for God is not chaos, he is adaptation, harmony, and therefore according to this proposition is a begun being. Logic is logic, and what applies to the universe applies to God. According to this proposition there must be an infinite number of Gods. Every God must be a begun being, for in every God are those "marks of design," or adaptation, which prove a beginning.

Upon whichever leg you put the argument from design it falls to the ground. The existence of God is unproved. If you say that design *per se* proves a beginning, then it proves God's beginning. It proves that there are millions and millions of Gods; an endless chain of cause and effect. There can be no such thing as an uncreated God, unless he is an infinite chaos. If design proves beginning, then it takes chaos to prove no beginning. The eternity of God, therefore, depends upon the disorder of his existence. If you say, as logically you should, that the beginning proves the design, not that the design proves the beginning, then theology is equally checkmated, for it is impossible to prove the beginning of the universe and therefore the necessity for a God.

Evolution annihilates design. Evolution declares simply adaptation, which is the result of environment, and is perfectly natural. Adaptation does not make environment, but environment makes adaptation. You do not need environment plus God. Environment is just as capable as God, and needs no God. No one would say that it takes are act of God to make fire produce heat. No theologian would be so foolish as to assert that. Fire produces heat, God or no God. So environment produces adaptation, God or no God. God would be a useless incumbrance in the matter. He couldn't make it any less, any more, or any different than it is The adaptations are, because the environments are, and the adaptations are exactly as they are because the environments are exactly as they are. The least change in the environment would just to that extent change the adaptation. Where is there any need of a purpose, or tendency, outside of the environment? It wouldn't change the result in the least.

If you surrender to the environment as the sole source of the adaptation, and ask who made the environment, I might answer a fool according to his folly, and ask who made God? We should simply enter upon a war of words and leave the realm of facts. Facts exist and always will exist somehow. Existence must always have a form, and that form will be an environment. There cannot be existence without modes—that is, there cannot be existence without environments. The question, therefore, is not the origin of environment but of adaptation. What makes the adaptation? The environment altogether, and therefore God is entirely ruled out. He is not even a silent partner. We do not need him in any capacity. To the intellect he is a nonentity.

If this God, this infinite goodness, this infinite justice, this infinite love, exists, where is he amidst the awful tragedies of human life? No sign he gives, no word, no light, no hope. Blind and still are the heavens to every prayer; millions perish, and they cry to God, and no answer comes. The babe dies upon its mother's breast; the youth is slain before the eyes of his parent; the wife sinks outraged upon her husband's breast; the old man totters to the poorhouse; the storm rushes; the lightning strikes; the waves wreck; not a moment passes but tears roll from countless eyes; homes are desolated; the little cottage burns, and the palace flames with crime; the martyr bows his head; the despot triumphs and the patriot bites the dust; liberty is in chains and justice is denied, and love seeks the coffined dust. Oh, the horror and the agony of human life! Ignorance is bliss. We cannot, must not, know it all. It would make one insane. Oh, the torture of it! And where is God? Cannot he heal one wounded heart? Can he not strike one blow for justice? Can he not answer one prayer? Can he not take one grain from man's infinite mass of misery? Not one, not one. He is cold and still, invisible, wrapped in darkness. He is indeed a lie, a cruel lie, a damned lie—and the world will not be happy until his image is forever abolished. We can be happy without God, but we are only miserable with God; for what is he but the creation of our own disease?

And so to save this hideous lie, another hideous lie is invented, the lie of Immortality, the only possible salvation for the God of man's idolatry. Time condemns, discrowns, and annihilates God. Will eternity resurrect him and clear his blasted reputation? I am afraid not. Is there any guarantee that God will be more powerful or more wise hereafter than to-day? Can the infinite change and improve? If God is helpless now, why not always helpless? If the conditions of time defeat his good intentions, will the conditions of eternity be any better?

Where is the gain? I want God, if at all, for present use. I would like to have him give some happiness here and now. If we have to trust God to-day, won't we always have to trust him and be forever disappointed? If God must allow wrong and suffering and every kind of horror on this "bank and shoal of time," and he is infinite, and never will be more infinite, why is not this sad necessity permanent? It does not help God at all to put off the date of reckoning. We have a right to judge him by the present scheme of things. The lie of immortality will not make any more palatable the lie of God. In fact, according to popular theology, God will be worse hereafter—more unjust, terrific, and diabolical. We can stand his deeds of omission in this world, and be thankful it is no worse. But how about eternal hell-fire? The little band of saints playing on golden harps, whose music will be drowned by the shrieks of a million times their number—is that a vindication of God's justice and love? Will that put the crown of glory on his brow—the flames of torment and almost universal ruin? I had rather take my chances here, and be a sinner here under God's frown than a saint hereafter under God's smile. Bad as this world is, the heaven of orthodoxy is more evil still. There is some love here, and joy. We do have some human sympathy and are not altogether crushed. But what is the hereafter? A burning hell and a heaven more damnable still; for the saint hereafter is meaner than the devil himself, since without a twinge of pain he can look upon the eternal torments of his own child. Theologians lie for the glory of God, but they only make him a greater fiend.

Even if immortality were of advantage to God, or to man, there is not a particle of evidence to prove it. Like God himself it is merely an assumption, a dream of the imagination. No Bible and no church has ever given a glimpse of light into the infinite unknown. Death to us is a wall and human experience has never passed beyond it. We may dream and we may hope, and that is all. The Bible claims to bring immortality to light, but it is a claim that is absolutely worthless. The only proof of immortality is the resurrection of Jesus, and there is no valid historic evidence of this. There is no proof that Jesus was ever born, no proof that he ever died, and therefore there can be no proof that he was raised from the dead. Even if Jesus were raised from the dead there is no proof that anybody else will be raised from the dead, for by the assumption Jesus is a God, and therefore his resurrection would only prove immortality of a God, and not of man.

There is no natural proof of immortality. The dead are silent. All the love and all the tears of the millions living have never made the dead speak. No voice is heard from the illimitable deeps. The best and the wisest stand at the grave in utter ignorance. Let us accept the fact bravely and patiently. Why utter a lie? We know this life, and we can know nothing beyond. Death is an awful tragedy. We cannot escape it; and we can not make it any the less a tragedy. We can cover the grave with flowers, but only the light of this world falls upon those beaming tokens. We see no angel springing from the sod.

As it is impossible in the very nature of things to prove the existence of God, so it is equally impossible to prove immortality. To affirm any proof of immortality is to lie, and this is the lie of religion—a lie to save its God from utter abhorrence.

How about the phenomena of Spiritualism? Does not that prove immortality? Well, if it did, the church, the representative of religion, rejects such proof. These phenomena are of the devil, say the priests, for the priests know that if Spiritualism is true, then their occupation is forever gone—for then immortality is no longer a matter of faith, but of knowledge, and knowledge is the eternal foe of the priest.

A scientific belief in immortality, as I have already said, is entirely different from a religious belief. They are really opposed to each other.

I do not deny the phenomena of Spiritualism. They have been asserted by too many honest and intelligent people, and the explanation offered by the Spiritualist is a very good "working hypothesis."

But is it any more than a working hypothesis? And is it therefore knowledge? Is it not a belief, a belief founded on evidence, a reasonable belief if you will, but is it, and can it ever be, more than a belief?

I ask my Spiritualist friend—that is, if he is a secular and scientific Spiritualist—to be candid in this matter. Of course I do not expect candor from a religious Spiritualist, for like all other religious people he will not reason. He will simply assume.

Admitting all the phenomena of Spiritualism, what does it prove at the most? It proves the present existence of an invisible spiritual world in contact with this present visible material world.

Is not this all?

The scientific Spiritualist will admit that the phenomena cannot prove future *endless* existence —only *future* existence. Therefore even with Spiritualism the demonstration of Immortality is impossible. But I affirm that Spiritualism cannot even prove a *future* existence—only present existence. Suppose I see a ghost, an actual ghost; what does it prove? Simply that the ghost is now living; but it doesn't prove that the ghost will live forever, or even that the ghost will be alive to-morrow. We may both be dead, ghost and I, before another sun arises. Why not?

Now, if the ghost cannot prove his own immortality, how is it possible for the ghost to prove my immortality? Suppose I see a million ghosts, or a million spirits, or ten thousand million spirits, what does it prove? Simply that these ghosts and these spirits exist now; but it does not prove that they always will exist. It is therefore impossible to prove the immortality of ghosts and spirits. The fact that a spirit exists to-day does not prove that it will exist to-morrow any more than my existence to-day proves that I will exist to-morrow. To assume natural immortality for a spirit is just as illogical as to assume natural immortality for the body. Grant whatever the Spiritualist claims, that this visible physical world is surrounded by a vast spiritual world, with millions of spirits, wise and otherwise, in its vast realms, will any scientific Spiritualist tell me that he has a particle of proof that this spiritual world will exist forever any more than that this physical world will exist forever? Imposing and wonderful in power and splendor as this invisible world is, compared with the immensities of universal space it is but a wave of the sea. Ten thousand million years are but a billow on the ocean of time. What presumption to affirm immortality of any form of existence, spiritual or otherwise, that may come within our experience! Our experience is only finite, and must always be finite, and it cannot prove anything beyond the finite either in time or space.

The scientific Spiritualist must admit that with all his phenomena immortality is still only a dream and a belief.

The survival of death as we now know it, does not prove a survival amidst all the infinite changes of existence. We do not know what cataclysm may come when we have shuffled off this mortal coil. We may escape one shipwreck but it doesn't follow that we will escape another.

Honestly, my Spiritualist friend, can you guarantee immortal existence? Assuredly not. You can only guarantee a continued existence, but who knows but what a spirit hereafter is as liable to death as this body to-day?

Therefore search the universe; listen to the voices of a million spirits; hear the symphonies of angels and archangels; and yet there is not one particle of proof of immortality. Therefore to assert proof of immortality is a lie and must be a lie equally with God himself.

Religion is not satisfied with what Spiritualism can scientifically give—continued existence. It desires endless existence, absolute immortality; such is its spiritual greed and colossal egotism. Tell the religious man that he will live ten million years in heaven and play on a golden harp and wear a crown and be happy, but that at the end of that immense period he will sink into nothingness; why, the religious man will be perfectly miserable. He will say all is vanity and vexation of spirit. Only ten million years. That won't do. I must have eternity. That is the everlasting cry of the supremely egoistic man, the cry of religion.

I want it understood that between religion and common-sense Spiritualism there is no identity in any way.

It will thus be seen how radically identical are the dogmas of God and Immortality. Without God there is no Immortality, and without Immortality there is no God. God needs Immortality to save his reputation, and Immortality needs God as its only possible guarantee, for only an infinite God can make endless existence certain to a finite being.

These are twin lies born of religion, born of a disease. They are not the beautiful gifts of science, the radiance of health, but the huge symptoms of an abnormal desire—the imagery of "life's fitful fever." But worse still, religion has not only made these lies professedly for the sake of human happiness, but out of these lies it has created the monster Fear. Religion has made cowards of mankind. It has made multitudes bend the knee in superstitious terror. It has made them slaves of king and priest. Of all the curses of which religion is the source, the greatest of all is this curse of fear, out of which comes the cowardice and hypocrisy of the world. Who does not hate the hypocrite? and yet the hypocrite is the direct offspring of religion. Who does not contemn the coward? and yet religion is the mother of cowardice. If those who are really religious by temperament and nature were simply satisfied with being religious and would let the rest of mankind—the large majority of mankind—abide in non-religious, every-day, comfortable well-being, I would not take time to attack it. But such is the nature of religion that it imperiously draws the sword, and would compel all the world to be religious likewise—in outward form at least, if not in real sentiment. But not satisfied with the sword, with the dungeon, with the fagot, with the thumbscrew, with all the cunning appliances for bodily torture, with devilish and supreme ingenuity religion has endeavored to torture with spiritual agonies, and it has terrifically succeeded. The bodily torture of man sinks into insignificance almost when compared with the mental torture, the awful fear, which religion has inflicted, in order that its own power may be unassailable. It has invented God and immortality, worse than a million thumbscrews, more hideous than the dungeon-house, more dreadful than a flaming sword. This God, the God of love, of justice—so called—this God, according to religion, is a God of wrath, a terrible war-God, a destroyer, a devil and a fiend beyond words to picture. He creates a heaven in the midst of infinite despair. He plunges the vast majority of the human race into eternal hell; he separates parent and child, brother and sister, wife and husband, and compels the one to sing praises for the damnation of the other. He makes the universe a tremendous prison-house. He makes man a slave, a machine, chained to a miserable doom whether he is lost or saved. For what is salvation but the picture of an eternal hell from whence we have barely escaped—"a brand plucked from the burning?" Thus God, who should be infinite justice and infinite love, is transformed to infinite hate and infinite wrong, and immortality that might be a beauteous dream becomes an endless horror, a stupendous scene of cruelty, of malignity, of crime; and so fear, the vilest, the most debasing, the most bitter fruit of religion, is born in the human heart, and this fair earth itself becomes a dim vast vale of tears. Death is the king of terrors, instead of a sweet rest in nature's bosom. Life is a torment, for duty loses its tenderness and becomes a barren path—merely obedience to a tyrant's will. Virtue is stripped of its bloom and beauty and becomes a slavish struggle for the salvation of the "soul"—the "soul," a lie born also of the nightmare of religion. For there is no "soul" any more than there is a God. Who can measure the damnable nature of religion in thus making eternity itself the instrument of its unutterable agonies?

I do not deny immortality—I do not know. But

if you believe in immortality; believe in that which is beautiful and glorious; believe in eternal hope and eternal progress; believe in that which is the bloom and blossom of all that is best and noblest here; believe in the triumph of sweet human virtues and tender human loves; in the triumph of liberty, of justice, of nobility, of generosity; believe in that which will give consolation amidst the struggles and disappointments of this life; believe in beauty, goodness, truth unending—believe in these things if you will, but do not believe in the hell and heaven, the God and devil, of religion. If you must, out of human weakness, fling a picture beyond the grave, let it be a picture entrancing with all the shining qualities that make this life itself so splendid. Let it give you courage to be more manly, more upright; to have a heart for any fate; but do not accept in cringing terror, with a slave's mind, with craven spirit, the heaven that religion promises—a heaven not fit for a civilized human being—fit only for a savage. A heaven which floats on the bosom of hell, is supported by hell, is really only the supplement of hell, and without hell would cease to be.

The God of heaven, the God of religion—what a colossal pauper he is! Did you ever think of it? What a beggar God is, and only a beggar—begging even the widow's mite; yea, and taking the widow's mite without compunction. Look at the army of beggars, all over the world, begging for the king of kings. An innumerable army. Tramp, tramp, tramp—no end to the procession. There's the mitered pope—a beggar always. There's the bishop, the archbishop, the cardinal, the priest—all beggars. There's a hundred thousand clergymen beggars, all begging for God. Churches, altars, incense, music, painted windows—all are for the purpose of begging, begging for this great pauper of the skies. And what has he done for man—this beggar on a throne? Nothing. He has not given mankind one fact, one ray of light, one invention, one discovery. He has not healed one ill of human life. He has never stopped a crime or punished a crime. He has never made one blade of grass to grow, or one rose to bloom. He has never soothed one fevered brow. He has never saved from disease, from conflagration, from the storm and battle. He has never furnished food, shelter, or clothing to starving, naked, and perishing millions. He has done nothing, this tinseled monarch of the skies, and yet he begs continually. He is reduced to such extremities that he can put only one oyster in his church soup; he must even sell the kisses of fair maidens. He must resort to the grab bag, and raffle, and ice-cream (mostly starch). He must even gamble—this pauper God. Oh, the humbug of religion and the humbug of God, when he does nothing but beg, and gives nothing in return for the millions that are poured into his templed coffers!

Have I not proved my proposition that religion is a curse, a disease, and a lie—everyway evil and evil only? In its very essence it is wrong, and can only result in wrong. History will affirm all that I have declared, and to-day we have an exhibition of the cruel nature of religion—that it is utterly incapable of being civilized and must be abolished altogether.

I dedicate this essay to Congress out of the indignation of my heart. I should never have written it but for the most disgraceful act of the century.

The American Congress has bowed down in absolute surrender to this curse, this disease, and this lie, and closed the gates of the World's Fair on Sunday.

In all the history of man there was never a more cowardly, contemptible, and degrading act.

It is pitiful to see the poor savage bow down to his fetish, his little wooden god, his snake, or cat, or calf; but how infinitely more pitiful it is amidst the intellectual glories of to-day to see the representatives of a great people bow down to this monster curse, disease, and lie—stab liberty to the heart, and perpetrate an infamous crime. The only consolation is that like Mokanna religion has shown its hideous face, and from this time forth its worshipers will diminish by the million.

The working-people of this country now know that religion is their foe and not their friend. The mask is thrown off. The despot is revealed, the enemy of liberty and progress.

Behold the picture—the beautiful World's Fair. None of us will ever see its like again. It is an incarnate dream of beauty. It is a poem in manifold color and form. It is the grace of all the world, the flower of every land. It is man's masterpiece irradiating his long and toilsome struggle. It is the bloom of mighty centuries out of darkness, conflict, and undying hope. Behold its gorgeous panorama, its superb buildings, its shining domes, its spacious roofs, its walls and towers that fling back the effulgence of the sun amidst nature's sweetest scenes of grass and flowers and water. Oh, what loveliness for man to enjoy. What a blessing on his arduous path. What an ennoblement to his toil. What a reward for his countless labors on sea and land—art is there which has drunk in the glory of the stars—art which has watched the misty mountain-top, the sounding cataract, the gleaming seas, the budding rose, the spraying fount, the forest's green. Art which has studied the deep heart of man, and mirrored in lustrous forms and tender face, in colors sweet and varied, in melodies sublime, the treasures it has found. Science is there radiant with a thousand victories, bringing from East and West and North and South its unnumbered trophies. Industry is there, with its great arms, swinging in song, whirling in music, rejoicing in splendor, giving gifts to all. This is the World's Fair, the ideal city of man's brightest civilization, where beauty reigns, where delight smiles on every path and each scene is an enchantment. What a place for the weary and the worn, the suffering and the disappointed; not for those who ride in carriages but for those who walk the humble paths of toil.

Behold the picture over against this embodied glory of man's genius. See the dark and smoky workshop, the grimy face, the drops of sweat, the toiling arm; the dusty feet. See the lurid flames, the hissing iron, the huge machinery. Day after day it is the same, smoke and darkness, toil and dust, and sometimes death itself. Look into the homes of these million workers. See them crowded together in the gloomy tenement, no flowers, no sunshine, no blue sky, no refreshing rest. See the pale mother, bent and worn. See the emaciated child. See the fever and disease, the want, the hunger of body and of mind. See the bare table, the unfurnished wall, the miserable couch. See the cobwebbed window through which only desolation peers. See despair in a thousand faces. See the weary limb, the lack-luster eye, the drawn lip, the listless hand. See birth and death in mingling horror. This is the world of poverty; and labor, which makes magnificent the face of earth, is doomed much of it to find its reward in this dreary prison-house.

Behold those contrasting pictures, the World's Fair, and the world of labor and of poverty, and so close, that the one is ready to give all its treasures for the consolation and joy of the other. These hard, sad scenes of poverty and toil can be made beautiful with the glory and the enlightenment of man's greatest achievements. What a blessing, what a wonder, and what a hope for the terrible martyrdom of millions.

But, behold, between these two worlds, the world of art, of science, of music, of delight, and the world of suffering and darkness, stalks this cruel monster, this curse, this disease, this lie—Religion—and holding the sword in one hand bolts and bars the gates of this paradise with the other, and thrusts back into vice, into ignorance, into misery into despair, the multitudes whose weary toils have made possible this magnificence of to-day. This treasure which has been pressed from their life-blood is shut from their eyes, their hearts, their hope. They must labor in sweat and pain, they must go to their unlovely homes, they and wife and little ones pining for light and air, for some sweet glimpse of higher things, for the inspiration and joy of man's vast and splendid career, they must be cabined, cribbed, confined. Upon their dark lot presses religion's iron rule, and makes it more miserable than ever. Between them and the beautiful world which ought to be their inheritance, at least one day in the week, is this curse of the ages more detestable than Milton's picture of Death itself.

Talk of civilizing religion; it cannot be done. You may paint it and veneer it and ornament it. You may mingle it with philosophy and poetry and art. Amid the softening influences of progress one may forget its "scarlet thread," its path of blood; but its nature is always the same. It can not be made of any service to man.

What will we do without religion? is the cry. Can the world survive its loss? Yes, it can survive the loss of religion as it can survive the loss of the cholera, the smallpox, and the itch.

What will we have in the place of it? Morality and Science. What better can we have?

Morality without religion will be more perfect and beautiful than ever—plain simple morality—regard for one another's rights, regard for one another's happiness, universal liberty, universal justice, every-day morality, not hights and depths, not heaven and hell, but "on the square." That is the whole of it. Integrity, truthfulness, generosity, manliness, courage, temperance, what better can be found in all the ecstasies of religion? Don't trouble yourself with the "infinite" and "absolute," with the "general" and "the universal" or any "supreme being," but simply do your duty to the individuals with whom you come in contact. Morality is between individuals, not between ideas, nor between individuals and an idea, but between individuals and individuals. Morality cannot transcend the particular. Do the duty that lies next to you. That is all. Do not create out of your heated fancy any false relations between you and God. No such relations exist. We owe nothing to God, and apparently he owes nothing to us. If he does he has never paid it. It is for him to settle with us, not for us to settle with him. When he makes himself manifest as an individual along the pathway of our daily life, then, and not till then, will we consider his claims.

We can understand our human relations. They are finite and comprehensible. It only confuses us to import the God-idea. It makes darkness instead of light. To import God into morality is like importing God into mathematics. God would be an impertinence in mathematics. He is equally an impertinence in morality. Think of a mathematician trying to solve a problem by the aid of God. A triangle has certain relations with all other forms, but what "God-relation" has it? And he would be a crazy mathematician who would invent a "God-relation" for the triangle. What nonsense it would be to talk about the "attitude" of a triangle toward the "infinite." There is no such thing. It is equally nonsensical to talk about man's "attitude" toward the "infinite." There is no such thing. The relations of man are numberless. We may not be able to discover them all, but every relation of man is a finite relation, as every relation of a triangle must be a finite relation.

The God-idea is not only useless, it is injurious. It is demoralizing. It obscures reality. It gives us false conceptions of ourselves and of others. It is a mirage. Leave out God and study humanity. Know thyself, is the grandest wisdom; and to know thyself it is necessary to know others and to recognize always the relations which exist between us and others, and out of these relations to behold the perfect bloom of ethical beauty. Morality is the continuous expression of equality and fraternity.

Morality requires no temples, no altars, no ritual, no churches, no popes, no priests, no Bibles, no gods, no prayers, and no sermons. It requires no vast expenditures, no processions, no swelling music, no *Auto da fé*, no Inquisition, no torture, and no fire. It does not beg, it does not rob, it does not murder. It demands no sword, no miter, no crucifix, no pealing bell, no gorgeous pew, no collection-box, and no missionary fund. It demands only the common earth and skies, the fireside, the home circle, the genial neighborhood. It demands only the ordinary highway, the handshake and the good morning, work and happy play, the evening's gentle rest, the voice of little children, and the common sense of all. How happy the world will be when morality prevails, when no rights are invaded, when the the inevitable ills of life are met with mutual sympathy; when self-respect is the universal grace, ennobling each and all—the humblest with the greatest. Religion has blackened the world; morality will give it golden days.

And Science—what grandeur is revealed in that noble world. Science the victorious foe of religion and the glory of the human race. Science the enlightener, the guide, the minister of ten thousand gifts. In science alone is the true self-sacrifice, the real surrender, the absolute abandonment to truth itself, regardless of all consequence, all fortune, all good and ill. Religion labors for the subjective, thinks only of the subjective, is devoted only to the subjective, to that within, the ego, the self, higher or lower, as you may call it, but self still, and not truth, not reality, except by mere cnance.

Science labors for the objective, for that which is without, for simple truth, for reality, for facts. It surrenders to facts, to every fact, be it ugly or beautiful. The man of science does not seek personal happiness, he is not searching after facts that will please him. He is not endeavoring to gratify some ideal. He sacrifices that which is most alluring to his subjective being, in order to find a fact. The fact he accepts, although it overthrows his most cherished dreams. What nobleness of devotion. It is easy enough to give up houses and lands for the sake of truth, but to give up some inward glory, some dear fancy, some charming hope, some exalted splendor woven of poetry and music and delight, to give up a supreme joy, that which might soften and glorify death itself, to absolutely, without reserve, surrender this for the sake of truth, the objective truth, this is indeed the sublime self-sacrifice of man—impossible to religion; but it is the natural spirit of science, for no one indeed can be a man of science when he allows the least personal inclination to bias his judgment.

It will thus be seen that science and religion are diametrically opposed. It is impossible to harmonize them. The one is the very essence of selfishness; the other is the very essence of unselfishness. The one is subjective, the other objective; the one is pure egoism, the other is pure altruism; the one runs to a disease and a lie; the other is abounding health and magnificent truth.

How beautiful is the way of science through all the world's history. How gentle, how patient, how brave, how charitable in the true sense, it has ever been. How ready to help; how eager to do and to dare. It is afraid of nothing, of no dark depths or rugged hights, of no desert or wild beast, poisonous insect or serpent's fang. It shrinks from no efforts. It shirks no task. It dares suffering, persecution, martyrdom, and death. It has been imprisoned, and through the prison bars hath read the lofty heavens, and revealed their glory. It hath been chained and yet it has filled the world with light. See the million happy homes it hath made; all the jeweled harvest-fields that shine beneath its footstep. Behold its pathway over the seas, the white sail, the glittering column, along a thousand leagues of beaming waters. See it meet the storm with spirit undismayed. See it grasp the lightnings and these fiery couriers bear our message with the soft pulse of an infant through the vast chambers of the deep; see it conquer the invisible world and heaven's swift breath carries our speech afar. See the iron horse, more brilliant than the chariots of old, make the peasant's journey more victorious than that of a king; hear the click, the gentle click, of that curious machine which has done more to emancipate woman than a million prayers or ten thousand billion sermons under the auspices of St. Paul; hear the music of the hammer and the anvil, watch the breath of the mighty furnace, look upon the molten streams of red-hot iron, see the glorious shapes arise more beneficent than any archangel; behold the million spindles while delicate and superb robes appear to clothe man's nakedness, far surpassing the fig-leaves of Jehovah's Eden; handle the polished instruments that conquer disease and stay death, more radiant than the golden harps; see nature's wildest haunts and earth's profoundest caverns contributing their riches to man's enjoyment, and see the rolling stars, planets and suns, innumerable systems, orbs that perhaps perished millions of years ago and yet blaze upon our vision to-night. Ah, what might we not behold if we could analyze those brilliant waves of light, and read the message from those enormous and distant realms. In these constellated spaces science has unfolded a fairy world indeed, even as in the tiny film and grain of sand other worlds equally beautiful, as measureless to the glance, she unrolls in spacious scenes.

I would say, let Science reign, but Science does not want to reign. She desires no sword and no crown. Evermore she is the servant of humanity. Patiently she labors, scorning nothing, fearing nothing, hating nothing, and loving the truth.

What shall we put in the place of religion, the curse, the disease, and the lie?

I have answered it, and may the working-people of this republic whose rights have been so basely invaded, understand henceforth the true benefactor of this world.

ORTHODOXY.

Orthodoxy, in its very nature, is hateful. It has no redeeming quality. It is not true, and it is not good. It is simply and absolutely ugly.

It is born of the hideous side of the universe and of nature. It is the incarnation of fear. It breathes only of sorrow, desolation, and night. It abhors sunshine. It is a system of despair. It makes man a beast and God a devil. Its mockery of redemption only makes more cruel the horrors of the hereafter. Its Christ is a picture of weakness. He satisfies only vengeance. Justice is utterly overthrown.

Orthodoxy is the supremacy of brute force. It makes might the right. Its divinity is an irresponsible monster. He is under no obligation either to truth or duty. He can lie, steal, murder, and destroy; and yet he is to be praised forever. He is king of heaven, and he can do no wrong although he violates every sentiment of humanity.

Orthodoxy is the ally of tyranny. It has never breathed a word in favor of freedom. It has lighted every fagot. It has built the prison-house and the gallows. It has armed the despot. It has made bloody the pages of history. It chains the heart and the mind of man. It rules by terror. Submission is its law. To rebel is the unpardonable crime.

Whenever Orthodoxy reigns there is the clank of fetters, the cry of tortured victims, the bones of martyrs, the gloom of the dungeon, the flame of dismantled homes, the infinite havoc of war. There the child is torn from its mother, the wife from the husband. All ties of nature, of friendship, of love, are disregarded. Nothing is sacred to Orthodoxy but slavery Its only hope is helplessness. To do nothing and to be nothing is the road to heaven. To achieve on one's own responsibility is to incur the direst punishment. There must be no individuality, no self-reliance, no independence, no heroic action in Orthodoxy. There must be only humility, subserviency, the bended knee, the prayer. One must not stand up. He must be forever on the ground and put his lips to the dust.

Orthodoxy is relentlessly repugnant to progress. It is altogether conservative. It looks backward, and not forward. It has no faith in the new. Orthodoxy does not admit that there is anything better than itself, anything more noble, more beautiful. In Orthodoxy, there are no hights to gain. The universe is one dead level. History is an everlasting repetition, the treadmill of the beast of burden. It has no perspective, no pictures, and no anticipations. Everything is already acquired. The unknown is a myth; the known is only between the lids of a barbaric Bible. This is the "word of God," and it cannot be added to. Eighteen hundred years have passed, yet Orthodoxy has given no discovery, no invention. It has not increased one whit the area of human happiness. Its mockery of heaven has added nothing to the wealth of human civilization. The God of Orthodoxy has not plowed one inch of soil or reaped one golden harvest. If he made the world in six days, it so completely exhausted him that he has been on the retired list ever since; but he has drawn his full pay just the same, and his priests and embassadors have lived on the fat of the land.

Orthodoxy is the upholder and defender of poverty. It says, Blessed be ye poor—poor in pocket and poor in spirit. It thinks that poverty is the condition of virtue; that no man can be good if he is rich. It advises the poor man to stay where he is, to live in tenement houses—and lay up treasure in heaven; to submit to injustice, and toil for a bare pittance; cringe through life and creep through life; worry along till death comes, and then play on a harp of gold. Orthodoxy deals with poverty merely by alms-giving. It makes no plea for the manhood and dignity of the toiler. It has no appeal for justice. Intent on the skies, it forgets the actual sufferings of millions on this earth. Hastening to eternity, it has no wish for the amelioration of the worker in the fields of time. What is poverty, what is disease, what is starvation? Nothing very bad, says Orthodoxy, for all here is shadow. The reality only is on "the other side."

Orthodoxy is the degradation of this world. It pours contempt on all human affairs. It has no interest in what is simply manly, for simple manliness, according to Orthodoxy, is total depravity. The welfare, the interests, the happiness, the glory of this life is nothing. Orthodoxy disdains nature. What are the flowers, the grass, the running brooks, the blue sky, to Orthodoxy? What the song of birds, the play of little children, the voices of affection which finds in the present moment the transcendent joy? These are nothing to Orthodoxy. It turns from them. It looks on high, to the blank spaces. It awaits the trumpet of the angel whose blast is the destruction of earthly delights. It revels in the Judgment Day, when all those who find in human love, labor, association, and devotion sufficient motive and reward, shall be doomed to everlasting perdition. The whole purpose of Orthodoxy is to belittle humanity, the reason, the natural sentiments of man and elevate his "soul," which is so infinitely small that no microscope has ever yet been able to discover it. Orthodoxy stakes its worth, however, on the value of this vanishing point. The sole mission of Orthodoxy is to give a pair of wings to a nonentity. Everything else—art, literature, progress, culture, wealth, business, the simple home life—these have no attraction to Orthodoxy. All its energies, all its churches, all its ministers, all its disciples, are devoted to the salvation of a totally worthless, depraved, and undiscoverable vacuity called "the soul." All else sinks into insignificance in comparison with this tremendous undertaking. The chief advantage of this world to Orthodoxy is that it affords a starting-point for the little end of nothing

"To tower away
To raptures of eternal day."

Orthodoxy begins in ignorance and it ends in ignorance. It is therefore from first to last the patron of ignorance. Its learning is only cultivated superstition. The brains of Orthodoxy "run to waste, and water but the desert." All its books, all its libraries, are absolutely worthless. They give no particle of information. Orthodoxy is either the tyrant of knowledge or its destroyer. It abuses it or kills it. It does not accept it as a helper or a guide. Science has had to win every position by martyrdom. Orthodoxy has combated every truth. It has an instinctive dread even of the advance of time, and would chain the flying hours if it were possible. It hates the revolution of the earth. It would like to keep the sun forever in the west. It trembles at the orient colors of the dawn. It crouches in the gloom of midnight, and is the assassin of every ray of light.

FREETHOUGHT.

Thought is the most precious power of human life. It sweetens every toil. It ennobles every delight. It is the supremacy of man.

To think, to progress, should be the happy lot of all. This is the paradise of the world—not material comfort only, but intellectual advancement. Reason should be the commanding faculty. The head must teach the heart. In music, in poetry, thought must prevail or there is no harmony, no excellence. Truth is not only stranger than fiction, it is greater. To comprehend reality surpasses every flight of the imagination.

The soul of thought is freedom. Without freedom thought is impossible. The slave cannot think, he simply copies. In so far as he thinks, he is free. The shadow of slavery is the grave of reason.

All triumphs of thought have been the triumphs of liberty. No step of progress has been made except by freedom. No invention, no discovery, has come save by the untrammeled mind. All civilization is the flower of the emancipated intellect. Freethought, therefore, is the word of to-day. It is the word of progress; it is the word of hope. Freethought is the necessary condition of improvement. It is the breath of reform; it is the prerequisite to all sublime achievement.

To teach men to think is the highest function. To urge them on to freedom is the noblest work. Thought and liberty blend in eternal marriage and cannot be separated. The victory of Freethought, therefore, is the victory of all. It is the solution of every problem that touches the destiny of man. It is the ideal made real.

Our flag, then, is Freethought.

We welcome all knowledge, all the treasures of the human mind. Our field of labor is co-extensive with every human interest, work, struggle, and attainment. It is universal. It embraces the whole philosophy of life.

Freethought is the ally of virtue and morality, for without Freethought there can be no virtue and no morality. The preeminent quality of all action is free choice. To be compelled to do a thing destroys the nobility of the doing. The chained hand can do no heroic deed. The chained mind is equally incapable. Freethought is the fountain of all actual human good, of all generosities, virtues, nobilities, excellences, philanthropies, of self-sacrifice, honor, chivalry, devotion, truthfulness, and magnanimity.

Freethought is constructive. It builds. It makes happy and beautiful the pathway of mankind. Slavery disintegrates and annihilates, Freethought brings together. In free diversity there is noblest unity. In liberty fraternity grows. In liberty knowledge bears its most precious fruit. In liberty the creative impulse of art makes the world lovely with new adornments.

Freethought is peaceful. It abhors physical violence, for violence is compulsion. Freethought reasons, educates, develops. Freethought is science, evolution. It is the power of knowledge, and not the sword of persecution. When Freethought is established arbitration will take the place of war. Harvest fields will not then be trampled by the iron hoof of battle. Homes will not be made desolate by shot and shell. Freethought is humanitarian. It makes gentler and nobler the heart of man and woman. It makes better friends, better neighbors. It is sociable, charitable, cordial. It is good-will to good-willing men. It brightens the fireside and exalts the home. It dignifies the common tasks of life.

Freethought is forethought. It is the Promethean fire. It is the mighty providence of the human race. It makes the wealth of the present serve the glory of the future. The Freethinker is the poet, the artist, the inventor, the discoverer. The mental slave is blind. One hour is the same as another. There is no to-morrow. The dull present only repeats itself. There is no aspiration, no change. The Freethinker in the full enjoyment of to-day, creates the noblest conditions for to-morrow. Freedom is the mother of wisdom, of foresight. From the heart of what is it plucks the crown of that which is to be.

THE CONSTITUTION AND HOLY DAYS AND HOLIDAYS.

ARGUMENT BY SAMUEL P. PUTNAM BEFORE THE COLUMBIAN EXPOSITION COMMITTEE OF THE HOUSE OF REPRESENTATIVES, JANUARY 12TH, AGAINST THE SUNDAY-CLOSING CLAUSE.

So far as Sunday is different from any other day of the week, it is either a holy day or a holiday. If therefore there is to be any legislation concerning the observance of this day, it must be on the ground that it is a holy day or a holiday.

A holy day is necessarily a religious or church day. If there were no religion or no church there would be no holy day. Legislation therefore for the observance of Sunday as a holy day is religious legislation—that is, it is legislation for the establishment of a religious or church observance, and therefore for an establishment of religion itself. But such legislation is absolutely forbidden by the Constitution. "Congress shall make no law respecting an establishment of religion." Madison says that "religion is entirely beyond the purview of government." Washington says, "In no sense whatever is this government founded upon the

Christian religion." Jefferson has stated the unconstitutionality of religious legislation. In a letter Jan. 23, 1808, to the Rev. Mr. Millar he writes:

Washington, January 23, 1808.—SIR: I have duly received your favor of the eighteenth, and am thankful to you for having written it, because it is more agreeable to prevent than to refuse what I do not think myself authorized to comply with. I consider the government of the United States *as interdicted by the Constitution from intermeddling with religious institutions, their doctrines, discipline, or exercises.* This results not only from the provision that no law shall be made respecting the establishment or free exercise of religion, but from that, also, which reserves to the states the powers not delegated to the United States. Certainly, no power to prescribe any religious exercise, or to assume authority in religious discipline, has been delegated to the general government. It must, then, rest with the states as far as it can lie in any human authority. But it is only proposed that I should *recommend*, not prescribe, a day of fasting and prayer. That is, that I should *indirectly* assume to the United States an authority over religious exercises, *which the Constitution has directly precluded them from.* It must be meant, too, that this recommendation is to carry some authority, and to be sanctioned by some penalty on those who disregard it; not, indeed, of fine and imprisonment, but of some degree of proscription, perhaps in public opinion. And does the change in the nature of the penalty make the recommendation less a *law* of conduct for those to whom it is directed? I do not believe it is for the interest of religion to invite the civil magistrate to direct its exercises, its discipline, or its doctrines; nor of the religious societies, that the general government should be invested with the power of effecting any uniformity of time or matter among them. Fasting and prayer are religious exercises; the enjoining them, an act of discipline. Every religious society has a right to determine for itself the times for these exercises, and the objects proper for them, according to their own particular tenets; and this right can never be safer than in their own hands, *where the Constitution has deposited it.*

In his autobiography Jefferson also relates:

The bill for establishing religious freedom, the principles of which had to a certain degree been enacted before, I had drawn in all the latitude of reason and of right. It met with opposition, but with some mutilations in the preamble it was finally passed; and a singular proposition proved that its protection of opinion was meant to be universal. Where the preamble declares that coercion is a departure from the plan of the holy author of our religion an amendment was proposed by inserting the words "Jesus Christ" so that it should read, "A departure from the plan of Jesus Christ the holy author of our religion;" the insertion was rejected by a great majority in proof that they meant to comprehend within the mantle of its protection the Jew and the gentile, the Christian and the Mohammedan, the Hindoo and Infidel of every denomination.

There is no need of any further quotations to show that any legislation for the Christian, the religious, or the holy observance of Sunday is entirely beyond the legal power of Congress.

Every sentiment and every argument in favor of the observance of Sunday as a Sabbath should therefore have no weight with this committee, or with Congress.

The only possible ground left therefore for any legislation as to the observance of Sunday is the fact that it is a holiday or rest-day.

A holiday is for physical recreation ; it is a relief from toil; it is for leisure, or rest from ordinary vocations.

What has Congress to do about Sunday legislation, granting that it is a holiday or rest-day?

Simply to recognize it as a holiday—but beyond that the function of the national government does not extend.

To start right in this discussion I will again quote from Jefferson:

> Our legislators are not sufficiently apprised of the rightful limits of their power; that their true office is to declare and enforce only our natural rights and duties, and to take none of them from us. The idea is quite unfounded that on entering into society we give up any natural right.

It is the American principle that the government is for the people, and not the people for the government. If at any point government infringes upon any natural right at that point its action is null and void.

It is a contradiction in terms to say that in order to uphold the natural rights of any human being, the natural rights of any other human being should be invaded. The exercise of all human rights is perfectly harmonious.

Whatever legislation there is, therefore, for Sunday as a holiday, or rest-day, there must be no infringement upon the natural rights of any human being.

It is the natural right of every man to labor.

Government has no right to forbid labor on Sunday. If one chooses to labor on that day as on any other day it is his right to do so. For government to enforce physical idleness on Sunday is simply tyranny. Physical recreation, physical recuperation, do not necessarily demand physical idleness. A change of physical activity is oftentimes the most healthful physical recreation, or rest.

Government cannot enforce idleness any more than it can enforce sleep. As well command a man to sleep all day Sunday as to command him to be idle all day Sunday.

This point is well stated in the decision of the supreme court of California:

> This argument—namely, that for the benefit of the working people government should enforce idleness on Sunday—is founded on the assumption that mankind are in the habit of working too much, and thereby entailing evil upon society; and that without compulsion, they will not seek the necessary repose which their exhausted natures demand. This is to us a new theory, and is contradicted by the history of the past and the observations of the present. We have heard in all ages of declamations and reproaches against the vice of indolence; but we have yet to learn that there has ever been any general complaint of an intemperate, vicious, unhealthy, or morbid industry. On the contrary, we know that mankind seek cessation from toil, from the natural influences of self-preservation, in the same manner and as certainly as they seek slumber, relief from pain, or food to appease their hunger. . . . If we cannot trust free agents to regulate their own labor, its times and quantity, it is difficult to trust them to make their own contracts. If the legislature could prescribe the days of rest for them, then it would seem that the same power could prescribe

the hours to work, rest, and eat.—*Ex parte Newman*, 9 *Cal.*, 509, 518.

The Constitution of the United States plainly declares the manner in which the national government should legislate, or rather non-legislate, concerning holidays, or rest-days. In the Constitution Sunday is recognized as a holiday, or rest-day, and only as such. When a bill has passed both houses of Congress for the signature of the president, the president shall have ten days to consider it, Sundays excepted, says the Constitution. Sunday is not a religious or a Christian word. It is simply the secular name of the day. The Christian term is the "Sabbath," or "the Lord's day." By not using either of these sacred names, but using only the secular name, the framers of the Constitution beyond question meant to recognize Sunday as a holiday, or rest-day, only, and not in any sense as a holy day. The Constitution therefore recognizing Sunday as a holiday, how does it regulate its observance? It does not regulate it at all. It leaves the president perfectly free. It gives him the holiday, but it does not command how he shall observe it. It simply allows a privilege. The president can work on Sunday if he chooses; or play; or go to theaters and operas; or hunt and fish; or travel; or stay at home. If the president is a Jew in religion, or a Seventh Day Adventist, or a Seventh Day Baptist, the Constitution does not interfere with his religious convictions. He can keep holy the Saturday and work on Sunday.

This is an admirable example for Congress to follow—shining in the Constitution itself, placed there by the wise and far-seeing founders of this republic.

The moment Congress legislates concerning the observance of Sunday as a holiday, or rest-day, by forbidding any kind of labor, it violates the religious convictions of many of the people of this country. They conscientiously observe Saturday as a holy day. What right has the government to compel them to lose the value of the following day, either on the plea that it is a holy day, or holiday, or rest-day? This is a manifest injustice. Follow the Constitution and no injustice will ever be done.

In giving the appropriation to the World's Fair Congress does not undertake to regulate the observance of other holidays far more national, important, and glorious in their significance than the Sunday. It annexes no condition as to the observance of the Fourth of July or Decoration day. Surely, if Congress can leave the due observance of the Fourth of July and Decoration day to the discretion of the World's Fair commission, it can also leave the observance of Sunday to the same judgment. Congress does not regulate the expenditure of the millions given to the commission. It has the utmost confidence in the wisdom and integrity of the commission so far as the use of vast sums of money is concerned. Why not leave with the commission the regulation of Sunday? Are the commissioners honest and able six days of the week and inefficient on the seventh day? or the first day? As the Constitution left the observance of Sunday entirely to the president, let Congress be equally wise, just, and business-like in its treatment of the commissioners of the World's Fair—men selected for their preeminent fitness to carry on in all respects this magnificent enterprise. This is my argument, therefore, to the committee—that in the very nature of the national government, and according to the Constitution itself, Congress should not make any laws as to the manner of the observance of holy days, holidays, or rest-days.

The Sunday, therefore, whether it is a holy day, or holiday, or rest-day, is entirely outside of Congressional enactment. If there is to be any regulation it should be by municipal and local governments.

MAN, NOT GOD

READ AT PAINE ANNIVERSARY, BOSTON, JAN. 29, 1892.

Come, let us sing of human glory;
Of freedom, love, truth's splendid story;
The thousand years of toil and strife,
That make the worth of human life;
There is no god, there is no ghost;
No great white throne, or heavenly host;
These do not flash Promethean fire;
Or make men better, stronger, higher.
Search all the stars, and day and night,
There's not one angel gems the sight;
There's not a heaven in all the spaces,
The grandest there man's own thought graces.
Man's is the vast intelligence
That through the gleaming bars of sense
Penetrates and measures all,
From earth to comet's fiery ball;
That weighs a million suns, and knows
The pulses of a star and rose.
'Tis man we celebrate to-day;
Who's struggled upward from the clay—
The protoplasm of the sea—
The ancient ape who climb'd the tree,
And climbing rayed the first surmise
Of man's transcendent faculties.
O, wise ancestral ape, to climb
Was the original of the sublime
And marvelous triumphs of our race!

We're not ashamed to give you place
In the long line from whence we grew;
We grant the gift that came from you
Better than all the gifts of gods,
Or miracles of prophet rods;
Better than any prayers that rise
With altar's bloody sacrifice.
That climbing million years ago,
In the mighty forest's gloom and glow,
Changed fleeting foot to skillful hand,
The toes, to fingers—so the brain that planned
Could be expressive, translate to real,
To outward form, thought's bright ideal.
'Tis not mere thought that makes the man—
What's thinking, if one cannot span,
With mighty arm, the mystic line
Betwixt the brain and deeds that shine?
Man's mightiest thought is but a dream,
If through the hand it doth not gleam
In action manifold and bright;
In a wide world of joy and might.
Thought is but seed; the fruit, the flower,
Is the hand's resplendent dower;
Art, industry, the cities grand,
The golden harvest o'er the land;
The steamboat speeding like a star;
The engine thundering swift and far;
The lightnings sweeping o'er the wire,
Obedient to man's desire;
The hand, it makes the music sweet
That crowns all life with bliss complete;
It builds the gorgeous wondrous dome,
The arch across the river's foam;

It shapes the statue's glittering stone;
Gilds canvas richer than a throne;
The hand, so excellent, so brave,
Not God, but climbing monkeys gave;
And when we sing of man's career,
Our "poor relations" let appear;
Don't scorn them who in grim old days,
Through cold and dark and perilous ways,
Struck the right path whereby we now
Wear fairest laurels on our brow,
Whereby we win the gold supreme,
Beyond the poet's richest dream;
Remember that the grace we are
Flows from those motions wild and far—
Through them—in Time long reach—we reign.
Why treat the monkey with disdain?
Huxley declares, I'd rather be
The monkey in that ancient tree,
Trying for higher liberty,
Than in this age of ample search
To be a bishop in the church,
Who sneers with theologic grin,
At those who strive some truth to win;
Who preaches sin and Adam's fall,
Eternal hell for nearly all;
But patient Science, wise and keen,
Its message flouts with scornful mien.

Let us take truth, for truth is great;
Let us see man in lowly state;
Brute, savage, speechless, naked, cold;
In forest, cave, yet ever bold;
Through infinite pathways gathering power,

Till centuries give their beauteous flower.
See, mystic India's gorgeous realm;
See, Persia shining at the helm;
See, Egypt's strange and splendid land;
See, Greece's master mind and hand;
See, Rome's imperial standard fly—
A hundred nations 'neath it lie;
Arabia's bloom of genius shines
O'er the dark years where freedom pines;
Then German vigor leaps to front,
Changes the world with battle's brunt,
While Shakspere's brain and Voltaire's pen
Make new and brighter fields again.
Along the shining march of time,
And broadening forth in dawn sublime,
Columbia, with her starry folds,
The promise of the future holds.
Yet mingling with the fair and glorious,
Mingling with deeds sublime, victorious,
Are blood and tears, the tyrant's blow;
The stake, the prison, crime, and woe;
Truth crushed and falsehood blazoned high;
Sweet fields laid waste while millions die;
Like beast, man grovels in the dust;
Creates a god and fears his lust;
Makes hell himself, and dreads its fire,
And murders every bright desire;
A slave—a wretch—he dares not turn,
And his own savage idols burn;
Blood-red the earth, and flame the skies
With incense, prayer, and sacrifice;
It is as if the brutal blood
Of dark ancestry rolled its flood

Along man's brightest, wisest course,
And swept him back with bitter force.

It is a struggle, life alway;
A struggle for the brighter day;
A struggle for the good and true;
It never ends whate'er we do;
Do we the best to-day, to-morrow
Finds its labor and its sorrow.
Let us work amidst defeat;
Climb the hight with bleeding feet;
Bear the flag though millions fall;
Answer ever to the call
Of justice, liberty, and right,
Though round us rolls the darkest night
Remember heroes, martyrs splendid,
Whose lives in star-bright glory ended;
Be simply true, by hell or heaven;
Be not to any duty driven;
Scorn all the gods, and love mankind;
Find courage in your own clear mind.

Such is the lesson taught by him
Whose crown of honor grows not dim;
Whose genius was the mighty power
That saved us in the perilous hour;
Who to a million hearts made way
For liberty's resplendent ray;
Who set the stars of burning glory
In our flag of wondrous story;
Defied the king, defied the priest,
And living, ne'er the battle ceased.
Sing him, sing him with jubilant strain.

THE STATUE OF LIBERTY AND THOMAS PAINE.

Before the mighty city, and beneath the stars and sun,
Where the flags of every nation sweep the air from dawn to dawn;
Where the New World opens wide its gates of morning's blue and gold,
To all the weary feet that come from crowded lands and old;
Moveless in solemn glory, grand and fair in storm and sheen;
The arm of LIBERTY sublime holds the torch by millions seen.

How beautiful it stands, that symbol of the splendid hope of man!
For which, on every path of time, the blood of martyrs ran;
The hope that broadens with each age from shining shore to shore,
Some gain is aade through every toil and every battle's roar.

Shine on, O, mighty symbol! the world must forward go,
Through vast and deepening conflicts ere it reach thy perfect glow;

Greet the sun and stars eternal with the patience
of thy fire :
Kindle still the dauntless thought and make firm
the high desire.

We care not for the hollow show that seemed to
mock thy grace ;
The farce of thunder and of speech before thy
silent face ;
What know these shallow-thoughted men of fashion
and of power—
Of what is in thy light to-day and in thy future's
dower ?

They spoke, with careless voice, of God, as if He
were thy soul ;
The Monarch of the skies—did he thy glowing
summons roll ?
'Twas man himself—'twas man alone—that made
thine arm so strong ;
'Twas man that flung thy flaming rays the cent-
uries along :—

Man—struggling man—whose spirit now within
thy face we see ;
Heroic man, whose arm will make the grandeurs
yet to be ;
From man thy beams shine gloriously—his heart is
thy great fire ;—
For man, to man, forever are thy splendors leaping
higher.

Thy marvelous form, great Statue! symbols him we
praise to-day ;

The man sublime, who stood like the brave warder
in thy fray;
Who bore, like thee, his torch aloft, and flung its
blaze afar;
And stirred a million hearts to deeds whose fruits
thy glories are.

Our noble Paine—without his voice, his pen, his
"Rights of Man,"
Thy form superb would not to-day defy the tyrant's
ban;
O'er land, o'er sea, thy coronal would not in joy
outray—
It was our hero's mighty thought that gave thee
this glad day.

Unlaureled still because he thought that liberty is
light;
That reason is man's noblest power—the morning
to thy night;
That king and priest are both alike the foes of
human weal,
That righteous liberty will not to God nor tyrants
kneel.

Fling out thy voice, O Statue! let thy dumb lips
proclaim
To ignorance and prejudice our hero's deathless
name;
Speak forth the truth, O Liberty! speak justice to
mankind,
And let the heedless multitude the world's true
saviors find.

In thy silence, scorn the servers of the creeds that
should be dead;
In thy glory, teach us courage in life's forward
ways to tread;
Teach the truth forever beaming with new luster
and new gain,—
And in thy scroll of honor write sublime the name
of PAINE!

TRUTH, BEAUTY, GOODNESS.

WRITTEN FOR THE OPENING EXERCISES OF THE SILVERTON FREETHOUGHT HALL, OF SILVERTON, ORE., NOV. 25, 1887.

To Truth we give this work of busy hands—
Fair Truth, that makes for life its happy toil,
For man his dignity, and for every path
The constant glory of to-morrow's gain;
Truth, forward looking, seeing in the old
The dawning splendor of the eternal new;
Reading sweet stories in the rugged rocks,
In wastes of sand, the darksome cells of earth;
In roots that struggle to the verdant soil;
In clouds that float along the endless blue;
The sunset's sea of light, and ranks of stars
That never cease their glowing march sublime.
Truth sees in low the glory of the high;
In dust the jewels of the golden sun.
Truth makes all things divine, disdains no worth
In man or beast, in clod or sparkling dew;
In cavern's gloom or constellation's flame.

Truth makes the world effulgent for the right;
Makes humblest duty an inspiring task;
Makes every work a fair and noble prize.
To seek the truth with every living thought;
To know what nature is and man himself;
To read the message of the rosy dawns;
To stoop and find the secret of the flower;
To see decay still ever flow to life;
And life in death still blooming to new grace—
This is our labor and our rich reward.

To Beauty, too, we dedicate our work.
Beauty and Truth, these make one living soul
In the eternal progress of mankind.
We would make beautiful the fields of life,
And in the heart of nature find the joy
Which makes the music for our onward steps.
We would make flowers for every happy home;
O'er every fireside fling the vivid light
Of wonder and romance—of hopes and dreams
That fact will always weave in mystery's web;
Hanging sweet pictures o'er our bounded way,
From the untraveled future's endless wealth.
Ah, swift imagination is not dead,
Though with the truth we walk the solid earth.
For truth is movement, movement is delight,
And in the brain of man is rhythmic power;
That so the ocean of the human heart
Still rolls in melody, and skies are blue,
And ever thought pursues its glittering flight,
While pregnant fancy o'er the dark unknown
From radiant blossoms of the things that are,
Scatters the myriad seeds of what may be,

To bloom and fade, the children of our wish,
Yet making dear the fated path we take.
Yes, we will have the song sublime of hope:
The music of brave hearts, the cheer of toil,
The dream of poet and the lover's thrill;
The artist's glowing pencil, whose deft hand
From Truth's white luster builds the rainbow's arch,
Making all colors grace the bending heavens.

To Truth, to Beauty, greater still to Good,
We give this work. It is for human weal.
It is a temple sacred to the right;
It is for justice and for kindly deeds;
It is to make us better, nobler friends,
Helpers in toil and grief; to lend a hand
To every fallen brother in the race;
To give the cup of water to the faint;
To feed the hungry, make our home the spot
Where sweetest virtues shine, with welcome there
For every weary toiler of the world.
It is for honest labor—each for all,
And all for each on fruitful breast of earth.
It is that man and woman, equal, free,
Shall still in duty seek the wealth of love.
Truth, Beauty, Goodness—to these three in one
We give our work and all our heart and hand.
For these we labor—not with fear and doubt,
But minds elate; for 'tis our radiant faith
That man will choose the good and not the ill;
Take knowledge and not ignorance for his guide,
And do the right because he loves the right.
Thus will our temple be a brightening spot
Where virtue, justice, liberty, shall shine,

And brotherhood shall be the golden link
In joys and tasks and sweet delights of home.

DEATH AND LIFE.

IN MEMORY OF WALTER LESLIE GRIGSBY.

Thou art gone in sudden horror,
  From the faces loved and dear,
In thy bright and beauteous manhood
  Thou wilt no more appear.
We have lost thee, we have lost thee,
  In the starless gloom of death,
As the lightning in the darkness
  So thy spirit vanisheth.

Where is the God that loveth?
  Where are the heavens that shine?
Where is the angel telling
  Of the power that is divine?
I see no God, no heaven,
  No angel anywhere;
I only see the darkness,
  And the force that will not spare.

Mortal grief finds no sweet message
  In the shadow of the grave;
Death is death; and all our dreaming
  From its torture cannot save;
We weep and cry in anguish,
  And tenderly touch the dead;
But the heart is still forever,
  The answering light is fled.

Let us meet the fate eternal,
  In the courage of our mind;
Let us not in weak endeavor
  Seek for hope we cannot find;
We are human, we are mortal,
  And sorrow we must know;
But with steadfast spirit meet it,
  In truth's undying glow.

Strew the flowers' sweet fleeting splendor;
  Lay the precious dust away;
'Tis a sleep that knows no waking,
  No weary night or day;
There's no pain, nor any trouble,
  In that chamber's jeweled dark—
The surge of life rolls placid—
  It has reached the fatal mark.

Our prayers are unavailing,
  And worship at God's throne;
In ourselves we find the healing,
  In human love alone;
In the hearts that cling together,
  As we place thee in thy bed;
In the honor that we render
  To the unreturning dead.

Our hope is with the living,
  In this world still fair to see,
In the days that shine before us,
  In the duties yet to be,
In the truth that beckons onward,
  In the cause for which we strive,

With the thoughts that make us greater,
  And the hights which we arrive.

Brave comrade, thou hast fallen
  Bravely fallen at thy post;
True soldier of humanity,
  In labor's splendid host;
Thou hast won the victor's glory
  In thy youth, and resting now
In thy calm and peaceful dwelling,
  Glows the laurel on thy brow.

Sweet remembrance rays its beauty,
  In the sadness of this hour;
For he that truly liveth
  Gives the world immortal dower.
We bury not thy virtue,
  Nor the love that thou hast given;
All thy kindly deeds are shining,
  Like the stars which gem the heaven.

Life and death are strangely mingling;
  But we press unyielding on,
From the shadow to the sunshine,
  From the midnight to the dawn;
To the dead we give our blessing
  To the living service true;
For the battle never endeth,
  Nor the good that we can do.

THE GOLDEN AGE.

In the wide future there's a golden age;
Richer than ever gleamed on poet's page;
Where all that's excellent on earth shall thrive;
And the pure generous soul alone shall live;
Where weakness, misery, and narrow thought,
The stupid pleasures that are sold and bought,
The heart that's false, the spirit insincere,
The dark ambition and the soul of fear;
All these shall vanish in its vivid light,
And happy homes shall sparkle on the sight.
O, there are prophecies of this bright time
In many a burning word and thought sublime;
We feel them when the gorgeous springtime flows;
When Summer murmurs to its golden close;
We feel them in those deep and mystic days
Which flash and gladden in October's haze;
And winter's pure and spangling lengths of snow
Unfold its fairy visions in their glow.
O, nature comes from out the heart of love;
It's rich with joy below, around, above;
The universal glory flames in all;
In constellations huge and feathery ball,
Within, without, to purity and life,
The perfect wonder shines above the strife;
The earnest purpose makes the spirit bright;
And paradise is found in doing right.

SHUT THE DOOR!

DEDICATED TO GENERAL HAWLEY.—[Written in 1876.]

The pious commissioners let Dom Pedro and party, Prince Oscar of Sweden, and a large party of invited Philadelphians, rove around in the grounds and buildings all Sunday afternoon, and some of the novel machines were exhibited to them; but the thousands of poor people from the workshops of Philadelphia were forced to content themselves with kicking toes against the fence and peering through the pickets.—*Philadelphia paper.*

Shut, shut the door against the poor, the low!
They shall not see the wonder and the glow
That would to their tired souls a gospel be,
And lift them up to holy jubilee.
They shall not see the flowers, a silent choir,
Pouring sweet worship in the Sunday air;
They shall not see the pictures, statues grand,
The treasured pride of many a spacious land,
Whose art and joy and beauty all combine
To flash the highest, noblest, most divine
Of all that man can do, in visible spell
To comfort, cheer, console, and banish hell;
For all this glory must be consecrate
One day in seven to God, who made us great.

But let Dom Pedro in! 'Twill do him good;
He's better than the vulgar multitude—
He and Prince Oscar, and the invited few!
'Twill please our God to let them take a view;
For they are Princes, Kings, Respectable,
Untainted with hard labor; they look well;
They do not need to see the splendid show,
And therefore God is willing they should go.
'Twill be a sort of compliment to Him
The poor can't give, so dirty, tired, and grim!

In this Centennial year we loudly boast
To be a pious, saintly Christian host;
Our nation's reverence is indeed complete;
We worship God, Dom Pedro, and the *elite.*